Stress-busting for Teachers

Chris Kyriacou

Nelson Thornes
a Wolters Kluwer business

First published in 2000 by:
Nelson Thornes Ltd
Delta Place
27 Bath Road
Cheltenham
GL53 7TH
UK

07 08 09 10/ 10 9 8 7 6 5

ISBN 978 0 7487 5312 3

Cartoons by John Richardson
Cover illustration by Bethan Marriott

Typeset by Northern Phototypesetting Co. Ltd, Bolton
Printed and bound by CPI Antony Rowe, Eastbourne

Contents

Preface

This is a book for all teachers. All teachers experience stress from time to time. It's part of the job. Indeed, all jobs involve stress, some more than others. Being able to cope with stress effectively is a key skill all teachers need to have. This book aims to help you develop a range of effective strategies you can use to cope with stress at work.

In writing this book, I have drawn upon comments made by teachers in the many workshops I have run in schools on stress management and in the research I have conducted on teacher stress over the last twenty years. I would like to pay tribute here to the teaching profession. I have known so many teachers whose sense of professionalism and commitment towards their work is a real inspiration. Not only are they effective in meeting the demands made on them, but they also display good humour and a caring attitude in their dealings with others – pupils, colleagues and parents. I am convinced that a key feature of their success lies in using effective strategies for stress management.

Dedication

This book is dedicated to my wife, Christine, and my daughter, Helen, who have done much to keep my stress low over the years.

Introduction

Teaching is an exciting career which offers you an opportunity to continue with subjects you are interested in, to help children learn, succeed and develop, and to enjoy the camaraderie of working in a team. However, it is also a challenging and demanding job and from time to time all teachers will experience stress at work. Consequently, all teachers need to develop strategies to minimise the occurrence of stress in the first place and to deal with that stress which does occur. This book is designed to help you do this. The main focus of the book is on the practical things you can do to deal with stress effectively. In addition, it provides you with an analysis of our understanding of how and why stress occurs, and how this serves as a basis for developing effective strategies for managing stress.

Perhaps the most important point I can make at the outset is that stress is something that every teacher experiences from time to time. Indeed, it would be impossible to imagine how someone could do anything in life without encountering stress from time to time. Mild stress and occasional high stress occurs in every job, and helps spur us on to meet the challenges that face us. Indeed, much of the satisfaction people get from doing difficult jobs comes from successfully overcoming the problems which faced them. Some people even talk of the 'buzz' they get when they feel challenged in this way. Experiencing stress at work is thus both normal and healthy.

Why, then, the need for this book? There are some jobs, such as teaching, where the mix of demands facing you is particularly challenging and to some extent outside your control. As a teacher your prime job is to provide a positive learning environment in which pupils can learn. I have outlined the key skills involved in being an effective teacher in my book *Essential Teaching Skills* (Kyriacou, 1998). However, no matter how good you are as a teacher, ultimately it is the pupils themselves who have to do the learning and who have to behave well in lessons. You cannot *make* pupils learn or behave well; you can only do things that make this much more likely.

Similarly, there are many aspects of a teacher's work that can cause frustration. You often have to depend on the work of colleagues and you need time and resources to do your job well. Sometimes your colleagues or your conditions of work may let you down. Teaching is also about relationships between people, and one thing we know about human relationships is how easily they can go wrong, and how quickly people get upset when they do.

Teaching is the type of job where there is a real potential for high levels of stress to be generated on a regular basis. All teachers thus need to develop the skills involved in minimising stress. That is simply part of the package of skills all teachers need to develop and maintain.

If you are a student teacher or a newly qualified teacher, so much will be new to you that it is sometimes easy just to accept whatever stress occurs as part of the job. However, by spending a bit of time analysing why high levels of stress occur and what you can do to minimise stress, you will not only reduce your stress but you will also find the quality of your teaching will improve.

If you are an experienced teacher, there is a danger that having coped with stress quite effectively over the years, you will have neglected small ways in which the job has gradually changed, and failed to realise how certain aspects of your current practice may be generating unnecessary stress. Effective coping strategies are not something you develop once and then retain in the same way throughout your career. For coping strategies to be effective, they need to be continually reshaped and modified to take account of the way you have changed as a person and the way in which your work has changed. Without such a reassessment, you can start to notice a marked increased in your level of stress.

The book is structured to enable you to deal with stress effectively by combining an understanding of the stress process with practical action you can take to minimise stress at work. Chapter 1 focuses on how and why teachers experience stress. This chapter will provide you with an understanding of how your own perception of the demands made on you lies at the heart of the process which generates the experience of stress.

Chapter 2 looks at the main sources of stress facing teachers. All teachers have a unique profile of sources of stress. What worries one teacher may not worry another. However, there seem to be certain sources of stress which have been consistently identified by teachers. At the end of this chapter you will be asked to identify the main sources of stress for you.

Chapters 3, 4 and 5 outline the practical action you can take to minimise stress. Chapter 3 focuses on skills and approaches that enable you to deal with a range of situations in a way that will minimise any stress being generated. Chapter 4 deals with action you can take to deal directly with sources of stress in a problem-solving manner so that they no longer continue to be sources of stress. Chapter 5 looks closely at the subjective experience of stress, and the action you can take to reduce and dissipate the mental and physical feeling of stress.

Chapter 6 considers how schools as a whole can take organisational action to minimise stress amongst staff. This covers actions that senior mangers in schools can take so that the demands made on staff are organised in a way that minimises stress. This chapter also looks at how schools can provide a supportive climate for staff in which effective action to deal with stress is provided.

Finally, chapter 7 highlights the most important action you can take to deal with stress. That action is to make the decision to commit yourself to taking the action outlined in this book *now*. Whilst reading this book will in itself help reduce stress, you need to commit yourself to taking practical action *now* if the full benefits of reducing stress are to be achieved.

1 What is stress?

Over the last twenty years much has been written about the amount of stress experienced by people doing different types of jobs. Amongst the professions, teaching has consistently been identified, in study after study, as one of the 'high stress' jobs (Dunham and Varma, 1998; Travers and Cooper, 1996). The aim of this book is to provide you with an understanding of how stress is caused and to outline what you can do to reduce the level of stress you will experience.

It is worth saying at the outset that all jobs involve stress, and nothing can be done to eliminate stress altogether. What you can do, however, is to develop approaches to your work that will minimise the occurrence of stress in the first place, and to develop effective strategies to deal with the stress that does occur.

Teacher stress is not a new phenomenon

Stress in teaching is not a new phenomenon, as the following article which appeared in the *Schoolmaster* in 1879 makes clear.

A most distressing case of suicide occurred recently at Woolwich. The headmaster of the Woolwich-Common Military College shot himself on Saturday last. His brother gave evidence to the effect that the deceased had often complained that the work was killing him, saying that the trouble of teaching did not affect him so much as the worry of management. The case gives rise to serious considerations. Every now and then we hear of a teacher, elementary or otherwise, committing suicide while suffering from temporary insanity. What is not so evident to the general public is the distressing state of mind in which a very large number carry on their work. … The absurd anxiety to gain high percentages and outvie the other schools in their neighbourhood is the fruitful parent of many of the evils under which teachers groan. Overwork benefits neither teacher or pupil in the long run, however satisfactory may be the immediate results.

(*Schoolmaster*, 6 December 1879)

I first became interested in teacher stress when I was a teacher of mathematics at a comprehensive school in London in the mid-1970s. All the teachers at the school where I taught received a 'social priority allowance' in recognition of the fact that the school mainly served a relatively disadvantaged community. The main purpose of this salary enhancement was to try to reduce the high levels of staff turnover that were typical of such schools. Most staff in the school called this a 'stress allowance'. I was intrigued by this reference to stress.

Since then I have conducted many studies of teacher stress and I have run numerous workshops in schools to help teachers cope with stress effectively. All the quotations in this book (unless stated otherwise) are taken directly from teachers involved in these studies and workshops. The following comment well illustrates the mix of frustration and despair that is typical of the descriptions of stress given to me by teachers.

Stress produces very tired teachers, sometimes as early on as two or three weeks into the term. Teachers – my friends at any rate – are exhausted. I find that amongst my group, when people are tired they easily get depressed and at this point in time disillusioned. We are fighting a losing battle in coping with education cuts, we are regarded as a load of useless semi-academics who can do nothing but produce a generation of semi-literate vandals. Under this regard, when we are tired we give up. Myself, I rarely mark in the evenings or weekends – things are left, I am too tired. An attempt is made to catch up on long overdue marking at holiday times, but inspiration has gone by this time and it is a chore, but at least during holiday time there is time, peace and quiet, without the thousand and one interruptions of a daily school life. The point I am trying to make, although I'm sorry I have rambled somewhat, is that I am failing at my job because I am expected to do too much, and unfortunately I am not alone. I am failing because the job is too big. I know what I must do to correct it, make resources and think of alternatives – but we don't have the money to do this, and I still come up against the problem of a lack of books. My classes share one between three, and there are some books with pages missing, chairs drop apart. These are things which I can do nothing to combat.

Another interesting feature of this teacher's feelings is the sense of helplessness that is conveyed. There is a sense in which this teacher is almost resigned to the situation as being one that you can do little about. Although comments such as the one above paint a bleak picture, it is important to emphasise that there is much that a teacher can do to face the demands of teaching in a positive manner and to keep such feelings of stress to a minimum. However, it is quite common for some teachers to feel helpless in this way. Consequently you need first of all to develop an attitude of mind and an approach to your work that minimises stress in the first place. Secondly, you need to develop strategies that can effectively turn a situation around if, for one reason or another, the stress persists for a long period. These strategies will be covered later in this book.

A definition of stress

First of all, however, we need to be clear about the term 'stress'. The word has been used by many people in many different ways, but generally speaking most people would regard the experience of stress at work as something to do with the anxiety caused by having to work under pressure. The following definition is based on a detailed analysis of the nature of teacher stress developed by Kyriacou and Sutcliffe (1978a), and has been widely used.

Teacher stress can be defined as the experience by a teacher of unpleasant negative emotions, such as anger, frustration, anxiety, depression and nervousness, resulting from some aspect of their work as a teacher.

It is important, however, to be aware that the word stress is used in different ways by different writers. There are three main alternative approaches to the one that I have given above. First, some prefer to use 'stress' to refer to the demands and pressures facing a person, and to use 'strain' to refer to the reaction of the person to that situation. This is sometimes referred to as an engineering model of stress, where stress is seen to be the force or load applied to the system.

Second, some writers use the word stress to refer to a general level of challenge facing a person, both positive and negative. For example, starting a new job or buying a new house can involve a complex mixture of both positive and negative emotions, at times enjoyable and at other times upsetting. Such writers would include both the feelings of enjoyment and the feelings of being upset as evidence of stress. Indeed, some researchers, as we will see later, have argued that as far as the body's physiological reaction is concerned there is little difference between intense excitement and intense despair.

There is also a third alternative approach, which uses stress to refer to the degree of mismatch between the demands made on a person and the person's ability to meet those demands. Some variations of this mismatch model place particular emphasis on the person's perception of this mismatch, rather than any type of objective assessment of the mismatch. They argue that what really matters is whether a person thinks there is a mismatch. These types of models of stress are often referred to as interactive or transactional models of stress.

However, the vast majority of writers use the word stress, as in my definition above, to refer to a negative emotional experience. This will be the meaning of stress that will be used throughout this book.

Over the last twenty years, many people have expressed a concern about the high level of stress reported by teachers. Indeed, a number of government reports have highlighted the levels of stress experienced by teachers and considered what teachers can do individually and what schools can do collectively to minimise teacher stress (see, for example, Education Service Advisory Committee, 1998). In addition, most of the teacher unions have produced reports and booklets of guidance on teacher stress and its management.

A high level of stress in teaching can have a host of unfortunate consequences. It can lower a teacher's morale and undermine their ability to convey an enthusiasm for teaching. Teacher stress may undermine the quality of your teaching in two main ways. First, if you find teaching stressful over a long period it may start to undermine your satisfaction with the work, and may lead to your becoming disaffected with teaching. This is likely to have some impact on the time and effort you are prepared to give to the quality of your teaching. Second, when you experience stress this can undermine the quality of your interaction with pupils in the classroom. Effective teaching very much depends on a positive classroom climate, and, in particular, on a good rapport with pupils, coupled with supporting and encouraging pupils' efforts. When you experience stress, that generosity of spirit towards pupils, which contributes to a positive classroom climate, can disappear, and you may react to problems and difficulties in a less well tempered or, even worse, in an openly hostile manner. Being able to deal effectively with stress will help you to maintain a high quality of teaching.

Another major concern with high levels of stress in teaching is that if stress is experienced over a long period it can lead to ill health. At the same time, stress at work is also cited by many undergraduates as one of the reasons that puts them off considering a career in teaching, and by experienced teachers as one of the reasons prompting early retirement.

The ability to deal effectively with stress at work is an important challenge for both individual teachers and for the teaching profession as a whole.

Common symptoms of stress

The experience of stress affects people in different ways (see box). Perhaps the only symptom of stress that almost everyone reports seems to be the feeling of tension. Other than that, the feeling of stress varies a lot from person to person. A distinction is often made between individuals whose response seems to be largely psychological (such as losing their temper easily) and those who seem to show more physical signs (such as getting mouth ulcers). For reasons that are not fully understood, everyone seems to have developed a unique profile of how they respond both psychologically and physically to the experience of stress.

For example, a study by Kyriacou and Pratt (1985) explored the different response patterns of teachers experiencing stress. These indicated that the types of symptoms teachers reported varied from teacher to teacher, and that their response pattern was also linked to some extent to their preferred coping strategies. For example, teachers who tended to feel anxious and who worried a lot reported that for them trying to be as well prepared as possible for the school day was the most important coping strategy.

It is important for you to recognise your own characteristic response to stress, as this can act as a useful early warning signal for you that something is causing you stress and that you need to deal with it. Indeed, strange as it may seem, many people do not realise that they are going through a period of experiencing a high level of stress until they notice that their characteristic symptoms have appeared. In many cases, it may be someone else who spots this first and points this out to you.

Common symptoms of stress at work

Irritability	Feeling tearful
Depression	Sleeplessness
Feeling unsettled	Loss of sex drive
Short temper	Feeling tired
Feeling off colour	Nervous tics
Stomach complaints	Mouth ulcers
General aches and pains	Indigestion
Compulsive thoughts about work	Panic attacks
Feeling tense	

Stress affects people in different ways

One of the concerns about teacher stress is that the sustained experience of intense stress may lead to stress-related illnesses, ranging from a reduced resistance to the common cold to, in extreme cases, serious physical and mental illnesses such as peptic ulcers and depression. In many cases the experience of sustained stress is in large part the effect of facing pressure on a number of different fronts, including both at home and at work. Most teachers seem to be able to deal with a few sources of stress in their life relatively easily, but there usually comes a point where teachers can suddenly sense that there is just too much to deal with and that they are being overwhelmed by the demands being made on them. The following observation by a teacher well conveys this cumulative effect of stress.

> I had a week off last year with nervous depression, mainly as a result of taking a very low ability class three times a week – appalling behaviour, noise, no suitable equipment. Stress for me is not all due to the school, as I have to travel sixty miles daily and I get home exhausted and there is insufficient time to do housework etc. resulting in more stress. Too many pupils have poor behaviour and are rude and that upsets me a lot.

Nevertheless, it is important to note that the link between stress at work and the occurrence of a stress-related illness is a complex one. In an extensive review of the literature linking stress and ill health in teachers, Guglielmi and Tatrow (1998) make the important point that a high level of stress can lead to a range of unhealthy behaviours, such as rushed and irregular meals, heavy drinking and smoking, and working late into the night with insufficient sleep. It is often the unhealthy behaviours that precipitate illnesses rather than the direct effect on the body of the stress itself. This is one reason why maintaining healthy behaviour during periods of stress can do much to prevent stress-related illnesses developing.

The experience of a high level of stress at work over a long period can sometimes lead to a state of what has been termed 'teacher burnout'. Teacher burnout has three main elements to it:

- attitudinal exhaustion
- physical exhaustion
- emotional exhaustion.

Attitudinal exhaustion. Teachers experience a lack of enthusiasm for work and a lowering of a sense of job satisfaction. This typically shows itself in an unwillingness to do anything in a different way if this would involve more time and effort being spent on teaching. Teachers may also find themselves increasingly less interested in pupils' work or in going to great lengths to help pupils do better.

Physical exhaustion. Teachers feel physically tired for much of the time at school. Such teachers will typically say that they feel completely drained of energy at the end of each school day.

Emotional exhaustion. Teachers find it very difficult to sustain a positive feeling during the working day. Instead the dominant feeling during the day tends to be a feeling of heavy resignation towards getting through the tasks in hand. The main emotion here is typically that of depression.

The following comment illustrates one element associated with burnout – the sense of withdrawing from the situation and just trying to survive as best as one can. However, the reference at the end to humour suggests that this teacher has maintained a more positive attitude and has not succumbed to the feelings of depression that are typical of burnout.

> The working conditions in schools are now a disgrace. The way to survive is to make minimum contact. I am old enough to remember better features: a pressure on pupils to work; good manners; strong discipline; a progressive scale of punishments; respect by pupils and parents for the teaching profession; support from heads and deputies. The present organisation is a pantomime. So I shall laugh – and survive.

It is worth noting, however, that much research indicates that trying to cope with stress by withdrawing and reducing one's commitment to teaching is often counter-productive (see, for example, Gold and Roth, 1993; Kremer-Hayon and Kurtz, 1985). The vast majority of teachers gain their job satisfaction from a sense of doing their work well. Any reduction in commitment that results in their doing their work less well almost inevitably produces a greater sense of stress, particularly feelings of depression, because in the final analysis what matters to teachers is a sense of pride in their achievements; if this is taken away as part of a survival strategy, teachers are likely to feel increasingly alienated from their work.

In a very interesting study of how teachers' attitudes develop and change as they progress in their career as a teacher, Huberman (1993) points out that for many teachers there comes a time, when they reach the age of around 40, that they reappraise their career, and get a sense of how far they are likely to progress, and the extent to which they are likely to realise the expectations and aspirations they held for themselves when they first began their career in teaching. Many teachers will be quite content with how things have progressed and will be quite happy with the working life they have developed for themselves. There are also, however, those teachers who can start to feel a sense of disappointment, and the need to decide whether they ought to settle reluctantly for the career they have or whether there is an alternative career path that will enable them to realise certain aspirations. This period can be a critical one for teachers in determining their whole attitude to being a teacher, and can also play an important part in determining whether they will be vulnerable to burnout in the future.

Some younger teachers seem to be very much aware of this early on in their careers, and enter teaching with the view that they are unlikely to remain in the profession for the whole of their working life. This viewpoint is expressed by the following teacher:

> I feel teaching is a young person's job. I am unable to see myself doing this job at 65 years of age. I want more money and a different kind of challenge during my middle years. I want to grow old gracefully.

If you are finding this outline of teacher burnout depressing, remember that the purpose of this book is to help you overcome stress so that you can deal positively and effectively with the demands of school life. Teacher burnout in most cases only follows from a long period of exposure to a high level of stress coupled with the use of unsuccessful coping strategies.

What triggers stress?

One of the most interesting questions about stress is what triggers stress in the first place. In addition, why is it that some teachers in a certain situation experience a high level of stress, whereas another teacher in the same situation experiences very little stress? Research on stress over the years indicates that the main factor that triggers stress in an individual is that they perceive some aspect of their situation as threatening (see Figure 1.1). In other words, there is some aspect of the situation that the teacher has appraised as representing a threat to their self-esteem or well-being in some way, and it is this perception that then triggers the emotional response of stress.

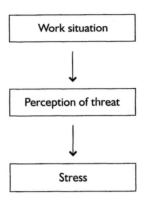

Figure 1.1 The perception of threat

This perception of threat may be in response to something that almost every teacher would agree is threatening, such as if a pupil suddenly became abusive and was about to attack you. There are, however, a whole range of situations which teachers will respond to in very different ways: for example having to address a parents' evening, having to get a large number of examination scripts marked on time, having to resist a colleague's demands that you do something in a certain way. Each of these may be perceived by some teachers as threatening, but not by others.

This of course begs the question as to why the perception of threat varies from situation to situation and from teacher to teacher. There seem to be three key elements involved here:

1 There is an aspect of the work situation that needs to be dealt with in some way or does not agree with the teacher's self-image of themselves as a teacher.
2 Dealing with this aspect of the situation is important, and it will have unfortunate consequences for the teacher if it is not dealt with successfully.
3 The teacher feels that they are unlikely to be able to deal with this situation adequately.

Stress is triggered by the perception of threat

Thinking about these three elements makes it clear why what triggers stress will vary so much. First, when faced with situations as described, teachers will clearly differ in what aspects of a situation they feel need to be dealt with and whether or not this agrees with their self-image. For example, one teacher might find a pupil's refusal to work harder as insulting and requiring immediate action, whilst another teacher might feel quite relaxed and unconcerned by the same encounter and not take it as an affront to their self-image as a teacher.

Second, teachers will differ as to whether they feel dealing with the situation is important and whether the consequences of not doing so successfully will matter to any great extent. For example, some teachers will feel making a good presentation at a parents' evening is extremely important and the consequences may be very important for their future role in the school, whilst other teachers may feel this task is of little importance or consequence for them.

Third, teachers will differ in how easily they feel they can deal with the situation successfully. For one teacher being assertive is something they find very difficult, whilst for another it is quite easy.

The teacher's perception of threat thus very much depends on each individual teacher's unique appraisal of what a situation means to them, and whether they feel they can deal with it successfully. In one very important sense, the perception of threat lies in the eye of the beholder. The distinction between potential sources of stress and actual sources of stress is a key feature of the full model of teacher stress developed by Kyriacou and Sutcliffe (1978a). What turns a potential source of stress into an actual source of stress for a particular teacher depends on the teacher's perception of the potential source of stress as a threat. In this model, shown in Figure 1.2, the term 'stressor' is used to refer to a source of stress.

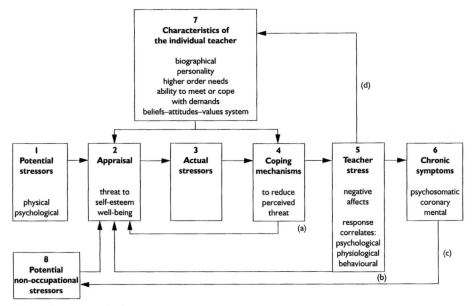

Figure 1.2 A model of teacher stress
Source: Kyriacou and Sutcliffe, 1978a

This model of teacher stress as an experience triggered by the perception of threat also helps to explain why teachers experience stress when no major demands are made on them. For example, a teacher may be very upset to hear they have not been allocated a particular teaching group they wanted. Models of teacher stress which are based on stress being triggered by excessive demands made on a teacher find this hard to explain, since this situation does not make demands on the teacher. However, in my model we can easily take account of this by reference to the fact that it is the perception of threat to one's self-esteem or well-being that triggers the experience of stress. Whilst normally this occurs when excessive demands are made, it can also occur when the teacher perceives an insult or when their wishes are frustrated.

Another important feature of the model of teacher stress shown in Figure 1.2 is the way the personal characteristics of the individual teacher, such as their personality, attitudes, and ability to cope with the demands made on them, have an important influence on the stress process by influencing their appraisal of potential sources of stress and their coping behaviour.

What is it about the psychological and biological make-up of human beings that results in the phenomenon of stress being triggered by the perception of threat? Broadly speaking, the experience of stress has its origins in the fact that we have inherited a biological make-up that responds to the perception of threat by preparing the body for a 'fight or flight' response in the presence of danger. Whilst the origin of this in other animals lies in preparing the body to respond to physical danger, in human beings this same biological response has generalised so that it is now triggered by any perception of threat, be it physical or psychological. We thus find our body making the same biological response of increased heart rate, sweating, release of adrenaline and a heightened state of alertness, to a psychological threat as it would do to a physical threat. Because it is inappropriate to then actually engage in a 'flight or fight' response, we are left feeling emotionally aroused and uncomfortable until our body is given time to calm down again. As we will see later, this is why learning not to see a situation as threatening is one of the most important skills in avoiding stress.

The model also includes four important feedback loops, shown as (a), (b), (c) and (d). The first of these indicates that the coping mechanisms used by a teacher may influence their appraisal process. For example, a teacher whose method of coping is to try to deny to themselves that they face any problem in the first place, may well fail to deal with new demands, and this in the longer run could lead to problems that are so serious that you are then forced to acknowledge them.

Feedback loops (b) and (c) relate to the way in which experiencing a high level of stress and associated symptoms of ill health can affect your appraisal process by making you feel much more sensitive and vulnerable to new demands. We all know how when we are feeling annoyed, tired or off-colour, new demands seem to be much harder to deal with and we are much more likely to regard such new demands as additional burdens which are seen to be threatening. Indeed, a commonly cited indicator of stress is that a teacher's usual level of goodwill towards others has disappeared, and that they snap in a hostile manner at new demands which in the past they would normally have dealt with in a calm and good-humoured manner. The fourth feedback loop (d) simply indicates that facing potential sources of stress outside the school can also increase the likelihood of seeing demands in school as threatening. For example, if a teacher is experiencing problems at home such as carrying out repair work on the kitchen, falling out with a relative, or having a child who is seriously ill, such problems can have a major impact by increasing a teacher's vulnerability to stress at work.

How widespread is stress?

When I first started looking at teacher stress in the 1970s, very little had been published concerning how often teachers experienced stress at work. Since then, there has been a huge amount of research conducted, and we now have a very good idea of how stressful teaching is as a profession.

One of the first studies I conducted was based on a questionnaire survey which included a question asking teachers how stressful they found being a teacher (Kyriacou and Sutcliffe, 1978b). The teachers were asked to respond to this question using a simple five-point response scale labelled from 'not at all stressful' to 'extremely stressful'. This type of self-report response scale has since been used by me in a large number of studies, and other researchers have also used this scale or one very similar to it. Typical findings in studies using this scale are shown in Table 1.1 (Cole and Walker, 1989; Dunham and Varma, 1998).

Table 1.1 Self-reported teacher stress

'In general, how stressful do you find being a teacher?'	% of teachers
Extremely stressful	5
Very stressful	20
Moderately stressful	40
Mildly stressful	30
Not at all stressful	5

About 5 per cent of teachers report that teaching is extremely stressful, and a further 20 per cent report that teaching is a very stressful job. The exact percentage of teachers falling into each category on the five-point scale varies slightly from study to study. There is some indication that the proportion ticking the top two categories tends to increase as each school term progresses, and to be highest (in the region of 30 per cent) in those studies where the surveys are conducted towards the end of the autumn term. This is not surprising, as many teachers report that feelings of stress seem to increase as the term develops. The autumn term is not only the longest term but also the term in which relationships need to be established with new classes, and the onset of winter brings increasingly colder and darker days. The school holidays provide a break which allows teachers to return to school at the start of a term relatively fresh.

Notwithstanding these slight changes over the course of the school year, the overall findings using this five-point response scale have been surprising consistent across a large number of studies and have consistently indicated that teaching is one of the 'high stress' professions (see box on p. 14). Other indicators of stress at work, including levels of stress-related hormones in the bloodstream, heart-rate changes, desire to move to another job and sleeplessness, all seem to confirm that teaching is a high-stress job (Travers and Cooper, 1996).

> ### The top ten high-stress professions
>
> | | |
> |---|---|
> | Prison service | Air traffic controllers |
> | Police | Doctors |
> | Social workers | Nurses |
> | Teachers | Actors |
> | Ambulance service | Journalists |

The one measure of job stress that does not conform to the picture that teaching is a high-stress job is that the level of actual stress-related physical ill health in teachers is lower than one would expect to find given the other indicators of stress at work. The evidence here seems to indicate that the long holidays between terms act as a buffer for teachers that helps their bodies to recover from the stress that has occurred during term time and thereby prevents the occurrence of physical illnesses to the extent that one might otherwise have expected.

Are some teachers stress prone?

Numerous comparisons have been made between different subgroups of teachers: young, old, male, female, senior and middle management, secondary school, primary school, newly qualified teachers, student teachers, teachers in special schools, and teachers of particular subjects. One of the interesting findings here is that the overall level of stress reported is very similar for each of the subgroups. In general, the same proportion of teachers (about 25 per cent) describe being a teacher as very stressful or extremely stressful. One of the reasons for this may well be the self-correcting nature of those involved in doing stressful jobs, which results in those who find the job too stressful either leaving the job or changing their role within the job so that they feel better able to cope with the demands which face them. We are therefore left in each subgroup with what is called a survival population of those generally able to cope, but with about one in four experiencing the higher levels of stress.

Research also indicates that there are general characteristics that make certain individuals more vulnerable to stress at work (Dunham and Varma, 1998; Travers and Cooper, 1996). In particular, there are three personality traits that seem to be strongly linked to stress-proneness.

I Type A personality

Teachers with a type A personality have an impatient, aggressive, striving disposition towards getting things done, and tend to overload themselves with tasks. These teachers are contrasted with those of a type B personality, who have a more laid-back and relaxed attitude towards life. Someone with a type A personality is likely to answer 'yes' to the following ten questions:

- Do you do most things (eating, talking, walking) at top speed?
- Are you usually anxious when engaged in a task to get it finished so that you can go on to the next task?
- Do you feel guilty when relaxing, as if there's always something else you should be doing?
- Do you find it hard to delegate?
- Do you find it almost impossible to attend meetings without speaking up?
- Do you get impatient with people who are dawdling?
- Are you physically tense and assertive?
- Do you interrupt people who take too long to get to the point?
- Do you find yourself often in a rush?
- When you are listening to someone else, do you find yourself tapping with your fingers?

The reason that those with a type A personality are prone to stress in large measure stems from their taking on too heavy a workload and thereby placing themselves under pressure. It may seem odd that individuals would do this, since by trial and error one would expect that most people would try to develop a realis-

Stress is linked to personality

tic workload for themselves. However, recent advances in our understanding of brain physiology suggest that some people can get addicted to stress. There is a buzz that comes from the high level of concentration and arousal that occurs when you have to work under intense pressure. Some of the chemicals released by the brain during periods of intense activity may, at a semi-conscious level, be felt as pleasurable, and, as a result, some people may come to continually seek out situations of intense pressure.

2 External locus of control personality

Teachers with an external locus of control personality have a strong expectancy that they have little control over important things that happen to them in their lives, and therefore feel vulnerable and helpless when exposed to problems that need to be dealt with. These teachers are contrasted with 'internal locus of control' teachers, who have a generalised belief that they have it within their own power to influence important events that affect them. Someone with an external locus of control personality is likely to answer 'yes' to the following ten questions:

- Do you believe that most of the important things that happen to you in your life are the result of luck?
- Do you believe that there is not much people can do to alter things that affect them?
- Do you believe that getting a good job is mainly a matter of being in the right place at the right time?
- Do you believe that there is little that people can do to influence government decisions?
- Do you believe that pupils' marks have little to do with how hard they work?
- Do you believe that no matter how hard you try you can't make some people like you?
- Do you believe that most decisions in life might as well be made by tossing a coin?
- Do you believe that what is going to happen will happen?
- Do you believe that you lack control over the direction your life is taking?
- Do you believe that examinations marks are sometimes very unfair?

The reason that those with an external locus of control personality are prone to stress relates to the fact that feelings of stress are enhanced in situations where threat is perceived and the person feels there is little they can do to deal with the situation. Since people with an external locus of control personality have a predisposition to see most situations in their life as being beyond their control, they are much more likely to see a source of stress facing them at work as one they are not going to be able to deal with. As a result, they will see the situation as being more threatening, and they will also tend to allow the source of stress to continue rather than to try out strategies that will effectively deal with the situation.

3 Neurotic personality

Teachers with a neurotic personality have a strong disposition to worry about things and to ruminate for long periods about problems (often hypothetical ones) that may face them. Someone with a neurotic personality is likely to answer 'yes' to the following ten questions:

- Do you find it difficult to get into a conversation with strangers?
- Are your feelings easily hurt?
- Do ideas run through your head so that you cannot sleep?
- Do you worry over possible misfortunes?
- Do you often feel disgruntled?
- Are you troubled by aches and pains?
- Do you get nervous in places such as lifts, trains, or tunnels?
- Do you lack self-confidence?
- Do you often feel self-conscious in the presence of your superior?
- Do you worry too long over humiliating experiences?

The reason that those with a neurotic personality are prone to stress is that they have a low threshold in seeing a situation as threatening. In particular, people with a neurotic personality tend to dwell on worst-case scenarios, and to think about how they would deal with hypothetical and unlikely developments. Consequently much of their stress is generated by thinking about situations which may not occur. Whilst we all do this to some extent, those with a neurotic personality take this to an unhealthy extreme.

Research in this area has also enabled us to build up a picture of the sort of teacher who can be described as 'stress-resistant'. Such teachers:

- are well balanced
- avoid ruminating on problems
- have a relaxed approach
- avoid overloading themselves
- believe they can deal with problems effectively.

Of course, most people who score highly on stress-prone personality traits will tend to avoid teaching as a career, because they know it will be a very demanding job. Indeed, teachers as an occupational group tend to have a higher than average level of mental health, in part because those with stress-prone personalities will avoid it as a career. If, however, you have a personality tendency in the direction of one of these traits, this can have important implications for your development of the coping strategies that will most effectively deal with stress.

In addition, it is important to note that there are also some personality traits which do not appear to be linked to a teacher's overall level of stress, but which nevertheless play a role in accounting for vulnerability to particular sources of stress. This further helps to explain differences between teachers in the sources of stress they report (Borg and Riding, 1993; Fontana and Abouserie, 1993).

As well as personality traits which are linked to stress-proneness, there are other aspects of a person's situation that can contribute to stress at work. One of the most important of these is whether they are experiencing stress in other areas of their lives. For example, during a period leading to a divorce or when you are having severe financial problems, the stress generated can make you far more emotionally sensitive to problems occurring at work. It is as though the trigger which causes stress at work is far more sensitive and the emotional reaction to a problem is far stronger if you are already experiencing stress at home.

Indeed, it is not just negative experiences at home that can make you more vulnerable to stress at work. A number of studies have pointed out that even apparently positive experiences, such as getting married, moving house, and organising a social function, can expose you to additional demands that undermine your emotional resources in some way, so that during periods of dealing with demanding 'positive events' in your home life you can become more vulnerable to stress at work.

Some researchers have developed a scale of life events and life changes (both positive and negative) which are used to assess the impact of such events on a person's feelings of stress which may, as a consequence, precipitate stress-related illnesses. A well-known example of this is the Holmes-Rahe Social Adjustment Scale. Taking the death of a spouse as 100 on the scale, other life events have been calibrated. The top ten items are shown in Table 1.2 (see Fontana, 1989).

Table 1.2 Life events and stress

Life event	Scale of impact
Death of spouse	100
Divorce	75
Marital separation	65
Jail term	63
Death of close family member	63
Personal injury or illness	53
Marriage	50
Dismissal from work	47
Marital reconciliation	45
Retirement	45

It can be seen from this list that three events in the top ten are, at least in theory, positive events: marriage, marital reconciliation and retirement. However, if three or four major life events or several minor life events listed on the full scale occur over a 12-month period, there is evidence that a person's vulnerability to stress-related illness is enhanced.

Another important aspect of understanding why some teachers may be more prone to stress than others comes from using what has been called the 'person-environment fit' (P-E fit) model of work stress. Over the years, a number of studies have used the P-E fit model to explore teacher stress (Pithers and Soden, 1999). This approach argues that one can measure the extent to which each person (in terms of their attitudes, values, interests, knowledge, skills and circumstances) is well matched to the demands of their working environment, and that the greater the mismatch, the greater the work stress generated. In practice, however, there are so many factors which influence the process of how much stress is triggered, that the P-E model is too simple to allow for accurate predictions to be made. In addition, it is important to note that teaching is not a single working environment. The working environment can vary immensely from school to school, and a teacher may find a comfortable niche in one school but not in another.

Nevertheless, it does highlight an important feature in this process. There is little doubt that some people are 'better suited' to teaching than others. For example, teaching is inherently a social activity, so those who feel less at ease in social settings and who rarely enjoy interpersonal interaction will be less well suited to teaching. Similarly, teaching is an exacting and professionally demanding career. You must be able to meet deadlines and to act in a professional manner. Those with a very casual approach to meeting demands upon them will also be less well suited to teaching as a career.

One other approach that also offers a useful insight into the stress process is based on the idea that stress can be generated by a person's perception of a gross imbalance between the amount of effort they are putting into a situation and the quality of the outcome that is produced. Van Horn *et al.* (1999) have argued that this approach, termed social exchange theory, is particularly applicable to teaching, as teachers often find that despite a great deal of effort on their part, some pupils, for one reason or another, do not perform well. The following observation by a teacher illustrates this point.

> I really work hard as a teacher, and I do my professional best to help my pupils get good results. However, there are days when I look at the work some pupils have handed in, and I really wonder whether all the effort I have made has had no effect whatsoever. You can lead a horse to water, but you can't make him drink!

Van Horn *et al.* point out that this applies not only to classroom teaching but to all aspects of the teacher's work, including administrative and organisational matters. Indeed, it is quite common for teachers to complain that they sometimes have large amounts of paperwork to do which they feel will yield little benefit. Clearly, this is another area where individual differences between teachers in their sensitivity to perceiving such an imbalance will make some teachers more stress prone than others. Those teachers who have a strong sense that their efforts should invariably lead to positive outcomes are likely to find themselves more prone to frustration and disappointment. In contrast, those teachers with a more realistic sense of the relationship between their effort and what can reasonable be expected as the outcome are better able to tolerate those occasions where the balance of effort to outcome is poor.

Measuring your stress

A major problem facing researchers has been the measurement of teacher stress. Self-reported stress questionnaires have been the most widely used approach. These differ a great deal in format and content. Some have included simple and direct questions, asking the teachers to report their overall level of stress on a response scale. Others have asked teachers to report the frequency and intensity of sources of stress and/or symptoms of stress and then computed an overall measure of the level of stress from these data. In addition to self-reported questionnaires, some studies have looked at physiological, behavioural and medical indicators of stress (such as absenteeism, leaving the profession, chronic levels of high tension and anxiety, sleeplessness, lowered sex drive, and hormonal changes over the course of a working week).

All measures of teacher stress have their strengths and weaknesses. The widespread use of self-reported questionnaires has been very successful in generating information about teacher stress, and has provided a suitable basis for model building and comparisons between subgroups. However, given the subjectivity involved in self-report, one must be very cautious about its use in providing information about a particular teacher's level of stress. Nevertheless, the checklist shown in Table 1.3 provides a useful indicator of whether you are experiencing a high level of stress at work. You should complete this checklist now.

Table 1.3 Stress at work checklist

Do this!

Rating scale
0 = Never
1 = Sometimes
2 = Often
3 = Almost every day

Rate how often you feel in the following ways using the above response scale (circle one of the numbers 0 to 3 for each item) and then add up your score.

1	I find myself worrying a lot about problems at work.	0	1	2	3
2	I feel work is affecting my home life.	0	1	2	3
3	At the end of a school day I feel emotionally exhausted.	0	1	2	3
4	Work seems to be one hassle after another.	0	1	2	3
5	I get very upset by problems during the school day.	0	1	2	3
6	I wake up at night thinking about problems at work.	0	1	2	3
7	I feel overloaded with the work that needs to be done.	0	1	2	3
8	I get tense and frustrated by events at school.	0	1	2	3
9	I feel my work is affecting my health.	0	1	2	3
10	I feel I am unable to cope with the demands made on me.	0	1	2	3

Score
0–4   low level of stress at work
5–15   moderate level of stress
over 16 high level of stress

---

2 Sources of stress

In the last chapter we saw that the experience of stress is triggered by the teacher's perception that some aspect of their work situation poses a threat to their self-esteem or well-being. There are, of course, thousands of aspects to a teacher's work situation. Only some of these will trigger stress. This will not only vary from teacher to teacher, but will also vary for the same teacher from day to day. A situation that occurs on one day may cause the teacher to experience stress, but the same situation on another day may not lead to stress.

Studies of teacher stress have indicated not only the main sources of stress facing teachers as a whole, but also how the main sources of stress vary to some extent from one subgroup to another (Dunham, 1992; Upton and Varma, 1996). For example, teachers in independent schools often cite the intense pressure from parents on them to ensure their children achieve unrealistically higher levels of attainment; teachers of children with emotional and behavioural difficulties often cite the unpredictability of the behaviour they have to deal with; student teachers often cite having their teaching performance assessed by tutors and mentors.

Common sources of stress

From the vast number of studies that have looked at teacher stress, there are ten areas that have consistently been identified as the most frequently occurring sources of stress reported by teachers (Borg, 1990; Dunham and Varma, 1998):

- teaching pupils who lack motivation
- maintaining discipline
- time pressures and workload
- coping with change
- being evaluated by others
- dealings with colleagues
- self-esteem and status
- administration and management
- role conflict and ambiguity
- poor working conditions.

We also need to remember, however, that every teacher has their own unique profile of what typically causes them stress. In addition, we need to remember that although these are the ten most common sources of stress, the main source of stress for a particular teacher may well be something not listed here, but which for them is their main source of stress. For example, one teacher told me that the main source of stress for her was having to take lessons for a colleague who was frequently absent; another teacher told me that the main source of stress for him was counselling pupils who were having problems in their home life. Such sources of stress may not be the most frequent, but for those individual teachers they were the sources of greatest stress for them.

Teaching pupils who lack motivation

One of the most frequent sources of stress reported by teachers is the frustration and exhaustion caused by trying to encourage, chivvy and cajole to work harder pupils who are simply uninterested in making an effort to do well. Many of these pupils are quite polite and sociable. They often do not cause the teacher any problem in terms of misbehaviour. However, these pupils are simply not motivated to do as well as they can. Instead, they will take every opportunity to work at as slow a pace as possible, they will be unresponsive when asked questions, they will lack the initiative to do anything other than what they are explicitly told to do, they will take every opportunity to engage in social conversation, and they are quite happy to hand in work that is incomplete and unfinished. One teacher referred to this source of stress as follows:

> A lot of stress is caused by the general lack of self-discipline in society being reflected in attitudes of parents and children towards school and teachers. More and more parents wish to get out of their responsibilities towards their children and transfer those responsibilities to the teachers. When I point out to some pupils that their work needs to be better, they seem to think I am some kind of alien from another planet – they are just not bothered whether their work is okay or not. Some parents have complained that the school sets too much homework, which I think is ridiculous. As such, it's no wonder pupils just want to free-wheel through their school careers. At the end of some days I feel so shattered by the efforts I have made just to keep my lessons buoyant.

Teaching a class composed of such pupils may feel like trying to run as fast as you can in a foot of water. Teachers often find that they have to exert extra enthusiasm and effort into their teaching in order to create a more positive and buoyant feel to the lesson. If there are at least a few motivated pupils in the class, the teacher's task is much easier, because these pupils' contributions and efforts can be used to sustain the momentum of the lesson. Teachers often say that it is the sheer effort of trying to animate pupils who lack interest that is the single greatest cause of their feelings of physical and emotional tiredness at the end of a school day. One teacher summarised this as follows:

Energising pupils can be demanding

Teaching → communication → concentration → stress all day.

This comment encapsulates the way in which for many teachers much stress is simply generated by the demanding level of concentration you typically have to sustain throughout the school day in communicating with pupils. Another teacher put it thus:

I love my year 2 class. They are lovely kids. I have no complaints really. But at the end of some days I just feel my brain is racing away simply because the day has been so hectic. I daren't drive home in case I go through a red light, so I just sit in the staffroom until I'm relaxed enough to rejoin the human race.

Maintaining discipline

There are two aspects of maintaining discipline that can cause stress. First, there is the level of alertness and vigilance that a teacher needs to sustain during lessons to prevent pupil misbehaviour occurring in the first place. This means that, with some classes, a teacher feels they can never relax. They continually need to be on the alert for a sign that there is a problem which if not dealt with quickly could lead to misbehaviour. For example, if a pupil is bored, cannot understand the task, lacks a piece of equipment to do the task, is having a learning difficulty, then any of these if not dealt with quickly could lead to the pupil's misbehaving.

The second aspect of maintaining discipline is dealing with the misbehaviour that actually occurs. This may range from quite trivial incidents, such as not paying attention, which can be dealt with quite easily by getting the pupil back on task quickly, using eye contact, a question or a soft reprimand, to very serious incidents such as a pupil swearing at you, where you may need to be very careful in the strategy you use to successfully deal with the situation, by staying calm, diffusing the atmosphere generated, and then asserting a firm course of action, such as speaking to the pupil outside the room.

For some teachers, dealing with discipline is not a problem. They have developed a high level of skill in pre-empting discipline problems and in dealing with misbehaviour. However, other teachers feel that asserting control is a very threatening situation. Indeed, for those teachers teaching difficult classes in difficult schools, very serious incidents of misbehaviour can occur from time to time, which can escalate into a heated confrontation, verbal abuse from the pupil, and on occasions even physical attacks. Clearly, for many teachers, dealing with such incidents will be a major source of stress. The stress generated by teaching badly behaved pupils is illustrated by the following comment:

> Stress in school varies considerably. Noise in one class does not cause stress, in another it does. This is because of the quality of the noise. A class that is noisy but working well (i.e. talking about what they are doing) is no bother. Classes that are noisily aggressive to each other make you wonder what it's all about and if it is a job worth doing. There is little stress in teaching, no matter how much work is involved. The stress comes from unnecessary paperwork and most of all from anti-social children who need constant disciplining. Fortunately, these are a minority, but they appear grossly exaggerated. I have one class of 20, with six very badly behaved pupils in it plus five noisy ones. They are virtually impossible to teach, utterly exhausting, and I usually spend my break after their lesson with my head on my arms on my desk and wait for peace and tranquillity to take over and renew my strength for my next class.
>
> I relax from school as I ride home on my motor-cycle and mostly keep school and home utterly apart. I forget the problems and tensions of home by working hard at school and vice versa. I suppose being a Jekyll and Hyde helps me to cope with both lots of tensions. I think stress comes from unnecessary worry and my philosophy is that I must survive so I set my sights accordingly and do not attempt the impossible. What is not done today might not be needed tomorrow, so why get in a sweat about it. I would say, personally, that if it wasn't for the above mentioned class I am not unduly stressed at school – but I do work break and lunch times to get everything done.

A study by Greene *et al.* (1997) focused on the extent to which particular types of misbehaviour by a pupil were seen by a teacher as disrupting their teaching. This study highlighted how misbehaviour is perceived differently by different teachers. Greene *et al.* argued that the amount of teacher stress generated by a pupil's misbehaviour is in part a reflection of pupil–teacher compatibility. For example, if a particular pupil persistently makes a noise in lessons, and if a particular teacher feels that persistent noise would be a major disrupter of their teaching, then that pupil's behaviour would generate stress, whilst with another teacher who is less concerned about such noise as a problem, little stress would arise. To understand how indiscipline becomes a source of stress for teachers, we therefore need to consider carefully the extent to which each individual pupil's behaviour is regarded by the teacher as a problem. The variation between teachers in what they regard as problem behaviour in large part explains why there are marked differences between teachers in how and when pupil indiscipline generates stress.

Time pressures and workload

Much of the stress reported by teachers stems from the combination of having a heavy workload and tight deadlines that need to be met. As one teacher put it:

> The main aspect of school life that is most stressful for most staff is the amount of work that they literally have to cram into one day.

Every day teachers need to be prepared to conduct lessons on different topics which take account of differences between pupils in their interests, motivation and abilities. If for any reason they are not fully prepared, or things crop up which are unexpected, the lesson still needs to go ahead. In terms of classroom teaching, there is thus a continuous series of mini-deadlines that need to be met. On top of this, there is a host of other activities that need to be carried out, including writing school reports, attending staff meetings, marking work, checking equipment, updating subject knowledge and preparing materials, all of which have associated tasks and deadlines.

Whilst establishing successful routines and using effective time-management skills can prevent many problems occurring, there will frequently be occasions where the combination of a heavy workload and the associated deadlines will conspire to generate stress. In such situations teachers simply have to meet the demands made upon them as best they can. However, in doing so, if your performance falls below the level of expectations that you have for yourself or that others have of you, then the stress you experience is likely to be high. In some ways, work as a teacher can be unforgiving. Pupils are likely to become restless or bored if a lesson is ill prepared; colleagues may well complain if assessments or other tasks required have not met the deadline or the standard expected. In that sense, you will usually get immediate, and critical, feedback if your performance is judged to be inadequate by others. It is the fact that your performance is continually exposed to the judgement of others that creates a pressure to perform well all the time.

Coping with change

The working practices of teachers continually need to change, to take account of external demands from agencies dealing with schools, concerning what should be taught, what teaching methods should be used, and how pupils' work should be assessed and reported. Continuous changes of this type are part and parcel of life as a teacher. Sometimes, however, these changes may be imposed so fast that teachers find themselves having to quickly give up ways of working that they were used to and felt were successful, in order to replace these with other ways of working that they may be unclear about and ill prepared for. In addition, the changes can sometimes be introduced in a way that strongly condemns the previous practice as out of date or ineffective. Teachers can thus find themselves trapped between criticism of previous practice on the one hand, and uncertainty about their ability to implement the new practice that is now demanded.

Coping with change can be a problem

Teachers are particularly vulnerable to experiencing stress when they have to change their practice. This is in part because their job satisfaction and self-esteem rest very heavily on the feeling that they are doing their job well. When a change occurs, not only does this require time and effort to deal with, but there is always the possibility that their performance will be less successful because they will not be able to use tried and tested methods. Indeed, if the changes are quite radical, such as having to teach completely new topics in a completely different way, then the adjustment required can be seen to be so great that some teachers will decide to leave the profession rather than go through a period of radical change. One teacher commented thus:

> The teacher's situation is probably far less static than comparable jobs elsewhere because of (a) regular change of curriculum and pupils (b) insidious growing of para-school care and administration (c) increasing logistic and resources restrictions by falling rolls and financial stringencies.

There is little doubt that the frequent changes which have occurred in curriculum content and teaching methods, coupled with the introduction of greater accountability and public assessment of teachers' performance, have generated a great deal of stress. Often, such changes have occurred at short notice, and have not been linked with adequate programmes of in-service training. This has meant that teachers have often been expected to acquire new skills and become fully acquainted with new requirements at an unrealistic speed. Moreover, many changes have been introduced in a manner that criticised previous practice and made teachers feel they were under attack.

Other changes can also be imposed on teachers, such as when schools are merged, reorganised or closed. Indeed, many studies have shown that school reorganisations that lead to experienced teachers having to attend a job interview for the first time in over twenty or thirty years, in order to compete for an appointment at the new school, can generate such high levels of stress that many of the teachers involved in the reorganisation will require medical treatment for the stress-related ill health generated (Kyriacou and Harriman, 1993).

Some researchers have likened the trauma of leaving a 'well-loved school' to a form of bereavement. Dunham (1976, p. 23) described a deputy head's experience of leaving a grammar school thus:

> She appears to be suffering from grief for the sights, sounds and even smells of the grammar school, just as, in community reorganisations, the people who move into new housing estates or blocks of flats grieve for the houses and streets from which they have been uprooted and for the people from whom they have been separated.

Being evaluated by others

The work of teachers is continually being evaluated informally by pupils, by other teachers, and sometimes by parents. In addition, teachers continually evaluate their own performance against the standards they have set for themselves, and in part with respect to how well they feel colleagues are doing their work.

As well as such informal evaluation, there are many forms of formal evaluation that take place on a regular basis. These may come about as part of professional development activities, including schemes of staff appraisal, and as part of external evaluations made by school inspectors or other outside agencies.

There is little doubt that a formal evaluation causes a high level of stress for most teachers. Certainly, student teachers report this to be their major source of stress, exceeding dealing with discipline and workload. Even experienced teachers, however, who are highly regarded by others, and who are very confident in their own skills, will report that being evaluated is stressful. In the case of experienced teachers the threat is acute, because there is always a fear that no matter how well you thought others regarded your teaching, there is the possibility that an external evaluator will be critical. Teachers have invested so much time, thought and energy into developing their approach to teaching that the consequences of critical feedback can be felt to be devastating. Indeed, the point is often made that almost all teachers have a strong disposition to take criticism personally, rather than to regard it as a criticism of their working practice that can be changed. The possibility of critical feedback therefore immediately represents a major threat to their self-esteem. This fear is well illustrated by many teachers during a school inspection, as the following teacher reported:

> My school has just undergone an Ofsted inspection, and I have never known stress like it. The whole atmosphere in the school was very tense and emotionally charged. Everyone felt they were living on a knife edge for weeks leading up to the inspection. I was really surprised by how nervous and anxious I became when I was being observed by an inspector, even though I am sure I am a good teacher. The whole thing was a nightmare from beginning to end.

Indeed, a number of writers expressed concerns about the high level of stress generated by Ofsted inspections and have pointed to these as a major cause of stress-related ill health in teachers and in prompting teachers to leave the profession. A study by Jeffrey and Woods (1996) of the stress generated by an Ofsted inspection refers to a high degree of trauma produced, and the strong feeling amongst the staff that their self-worth and professional integrity were being undermined by the whole experience. Studies of teacher appraisal schemes have also pointed to the stress generated during the period of classroom observation, both for the teacher being appraised and for the teacher doing the appraising.

Dealings with colleagues

From time to time, teachers will have disagreements with each other. This may simply stem from differences in views about how something should be done.

For example, there may be a disagreement concerning the best format to use in writing school reports for parents, or the amount of curriculum time that needs to be given to different subjects. In addition, sometimes a teacher in a more senior management position needs to encourage another teacher to change their practice, or may need to be critical of some aspect of their performance.

Most teachers, most of time, will be able to resolve problems and conflicts in a professional and positive manner. Occasionally, however, the feelings held may be so strong, or the problem may have been addressed in such a manner, that the quality of the working relationship between the two members of staff is impaired. If such feelings persist, then future disagreements between these two colleagues can generate further stress for one or both of the teachers concerned. Clearly many teachers have a close working relationship with particular colleagues, so if the two colleagues who have fallen out with each other need to work together cooperatively on a regular basis, the stress levels generated by this can be quite high. This is evident in the following teacher's observations:

> Far more stress arises from dealing with associates than with children or the task of actual teaching. For me the unfair behaviour of some of my colleagues upsets me a great deal. I find it really annoying when colleagues are unhelpful and will not cooperate with me on something I think is very important. One accepts that stress is related to one's own personality and psychosomatic make-up; one is to some extent the victim of one's own glandular type. Stress builds upon stress; stress is stimulating and can produce increased efficiency; one may even come to be dependent upon it for motivation. The demands made upon professional pastoral workers are becoming perhaps disproportionate. As a retired naval officer with six years' work experience, I was amazed at the excessive personal 'power of command' required to control mere 'children'. It appears to me that more and more 'power' is having to be 'turned-on' by teachers – and with it goes the accompanying stress. Those who are in positions of exceptional responsibility seem to go home often late (and to further school work) emotionally drained each day, to be exhausted and often ill at the end of term.

Self-esteem and status

Another major source of stress for teachers is situations in which their status or self-esteem are being undermined. Public attacks on the teaching profession by politicians or other agencies can undermine teachers' sense of the worthwhileness of their work and the esteem in which their profession is held by the public. Surveys of people's views of the different professional groups show that teachers are widely held in high esteem. However, highly publicised attacks on the quality of teachers' work can, in the context of claims about falling standards in schools, contribute to a lowering of teacher morale. This can also occur as a result of the more subtle undermining of the profession by the removal of levels of responsibility and decision making. For example, if teachers have in the past been able to make certain decisions about curriculum matters that are then taken over by government agencies, that implicitly undermines their sense of status.

Teachers often report that they sometimes feel that society does not fully recognise their efforts and the good work that they do, and that they are blamed unfairly if the standard of work that some pupils achieve is relatively low. This is illustrated by the following teacher, who is concerned that there are limits to what a teacher can achieve and that these need to be taken into account.

> I find the most stressful things about teaching are (i) the nagging suspicion that no matter how energetic, industrious or inspired one's teaching, it will in the final analysis have a negligible effect on the majority of one's pupils (partly for societal reasons and partly because of what schools are); (ii) the lack of certainty as to how successful one's work has been; (iii) the inflexibility and clumsiness of schools as the instruments for assisting children to learn about the world; and (iv) the pressure of what I can only call the philistinism and depressing ignorance concerning education of the mass of the public.

The introduction of league tables comparing schools on the basis of their pupils' levels of attainment has done much to increase teachers' sense of being judged unfairly in a way that undermines their sense of status and esteem. This is a pity, since the vast majority of surveys of the public perception of different occupations indicate that teachers are generally held in very high esteem.

In addition, at an individual level, if a teacher has a responsibility taken away from them for a certain task which they would have liked to have kept, then that may be felt to be a lowering of their sense of importance. For example, if a head suddenly tells the deputy head that she will no longer be in charge of organising the school prize day, the deputy head might feel quite upset about that. The trigger for the experience of stress here is the deputy head perceiving this as a threat to her self-esteem by undermining her self-image. If the deputy head is happy to give this task up, stress might still be generated if she still sees the decision as undermining her self-image. Indeed, on occasions some teachers will feel quite upset at not being asked to take on an important task, even if they did not want to do so. Again, what triggers the stress here is the sense that not being asked to do this task might indicate a low regard for their competence or role in the school.

Similarly, frustration regarding career opportunities can generate stress, not only for ambitious teachers but also for unambitious teachers. In the case of ambitious teachers, a crucial period seems to be when they are about 35 years

A positive self-image off-sets problems

old, and they begin to see how realistic their initial career aspirations are, and how difficult it will be to achieve them. It is often about this time in their professional life that many teachers come to terms with the likely limits of their further career development. However, even in the case of unambitious teachers, stress can sometimes be generated by not being invited to consider applying for a post of promotion, despite having no wish to do so.

Administration and management

Most teachers are attracted to teaching as a career because they anticipate that they will enjoy classroom teaching, teaching topics they enjoy, and helping pupils to succeed. However, teachers also have to carry out a range of administrative and managerial tasks in addition to their role of classroom teacher. Some of these tasks will be related to their pastoral care roles, particularly work as a form tutor. In addition, there is a whole range of tasks related to other roles in the school, such as organising school events, recording information required by outside agencies, monitoring budgets, appointing new staff and contributing to the decision making of senior management.

Sometimes, teachers will complain that they feel such tasks to be an unwelcome aspect of their work. Indeed, the expression 'This is not why I became a teacher' is commonly used by teachers to convey their sense of dissatisfaction with the administrative work they may be required to do. In addition, administrative tasks related to their own role of classroom teacher can also be heavy at times. Examination boards requiring more detailed criteria to be addressed when assessing pupils' course work, involvement in decisions about the composition of pupils into ability sets, and ordering new materials for teaching, can all make heavy demands on your time, and may involve difficult decisions having to be taken.

Some teachers may not like doing this type of work, and if it contributes to a sense of heavy time pressure and workload, it may generate a high level of stress, as is illustrated in the following comment:

> As head of a large department (twelve teachers) a great deal of stress is due to worrying about problems concerning members of the department and the running of the department, not so much due to problems with the classes I myself actually teach. I have only one administrative period timetabled out of forty periods in the week.

Role conflict and ambiguity

Teachers often need to exercise different roles. For example, as a classroom teacher you may feel that you may need to be assertive towards a pupil who is misbehaving. At the same time, you may be aware that the pupil concerned is having acute personal problems at home and is in desperate need of emotional support. In such a case, your role as a teacher who needs to maintain discipline in the classroom may conflict with your role as someone who has a pastoral care concern towards all pupils in the classroom. When two or more roles suggest different actions, a teacher is said to experience role conflict. If the teacher feels that such role conflict makes it difficult to deal with an important situation successfully, it will then generate stress. One teacher commented in the following way about the different roles that teachers need to discharge:

> I feel that most stress in teaching results from teachers trying to fulfil too diverse a role, which results in too great a workload with too little time to adequately complete it.

A number of writers have pointed out that the range of roles facing teachers can be particularly diverse for those teachers who work in special schools, where they can be expected to function as counsellor, carer, cleaner, nurse, social worker and liaison officer. Jones and Sharma (1996, p. 33) quote one special school teacher as saying:

> When I decided on the move to work with special needs children a few years ago, it was meant to be a positive move, but now I sometimes won-

der if what I am doing is teaching, really. I was trained as a teacher, but I find myself being expected to be doing things I never imagined I would be doing. I do sometimes find what I am doing is confusing, even disheartening.

Role ambiguity arises in those situations where you feel the tasks which make up a particular role and the level of performance expected of you in that role are not clear. There is thus a danger that others will be critical of you for not doing a task that no one in fact told you was expected of you, or that you will be criticised for poor performance when you did not know that a particular task was part of your role, or that a higher level of performance was expected. In order to overcome role ambiguity, some roles in the school will have a written job description, and the teacher who previously undertook that role will be able to brief you on what is involved. However, there are many occasions or types of role for which such information is not available. In addition, the nature of the role may have changed radically without your being informed. Teachers are often particularly sensitive to criticism, so that role conflict or role ambiguity can be powerful sources of stress.

Poor working conditions

Poor working conditions cover a host of potential sources of stress, such as a lack of adequate resources and materials, poor physical condition of the school buildings, inadequate level of support from clerical and administrative staff, lack of time for preparation, and a lack of opportunity for professional development activities.

Stress is particularly likely to be generated by anything which is felt to hinder the teacher's ability to do their work. For example, finding that the equipment needed to produce multiple copies of a worksheet is broken, inadequate storage space to keep pupils' exercise books, and too great a distance from the staffroom to the teaching room to enable the teacher to have an adequate coffee break, can all serve to make the school day harder for the teacher.

There is little doubt that in the context of heavy time pressures and workload, even a simple problem can generate a high level of stress. For example, you may have discovered a few minutes before a lesson that a tape recorder has become faulty. You need to decide quickly whether you can get hold of a replacement or should reorganise your lesson to do without it. If the class you are about to teach are likely to misbehave if the lesson is not well planned, or were looking forward to the particular task you were expecting to give them, this can increase the level of stress experienced.

In addition, the quality of working conditions can contribute to teachers' feelings of professional respect. The better their working conditions, the more likely teachers will feel that their self-image is enhanced. There is no doubt that 'being treated like a professional' is important to teachers. Conversely, poor working conditions that undermine this self-image can have the opposite effect. This is illustrated in the following comment:

> Some of the physical conditions under which teachers work contribute to stress, e.g. lack of noise insulation between classrooms, damp classrooms which haven't been painted for years, just unaesthetic physical surroundings. The school in which I teach is large and the staff are very pleasant but we do discuss this point and what teachers are required to put up with. Besides, most teachers now can hardly make ends meet, the current salary levels are very hard on those who have a few children. The occasional sabbatical could help teachers to refresh and revitalise themselves. It is amazing that the unions have not campaigned for this. I know several teachers who would willingly take a year to do something entirely different from teaching – even getting another job with pay so that they can have other experiences but have the guarantee of their job at the end of the period. It might broaden their vision as well! This sabbatical could be without pay if they have another job.

It is also worth noting that teachers often get physically tired if they have to cover great distances or climb flights of stairs on a regular basis throughout the school day. Indeed, they may even have to travel between separate buildings in schools which operate on a split site. Such physical tiredness can make it more likely that other problems will generate stress. Consequently anything that can be done to minimise unnecessary physical demands is also important.

Sources of stress for student teachers

A number of studies have highlighted the main sources of stress facing student teachers during their period of teaching practice in schools (Head *et al.*, 1996; Kyriacou and Stephens, 1999; Morton *et al.*, 1997). The top ten sources of stress are identified as follows:

- being assessed
- dealing with disruptive behaviour
- coping with a heavy workload
- getting the teaching right
- planning lessons
- dealing with responsibilities
- not being regarded as a real teacher
- modifying your ideals and self-image

- getting on with school staff
- teaching about sensitive issues.

Being assessed

A major source of stress for student teachers is the anxiety generated when being observed and evaluated by their university supervisor and by teachers at the teaching practice school. Most student teachers are very concerned about how teachers and their supervisor might react to seeing one or more unsuccessful lessons, and are particularly worried if they have classes where control problems are occurring. However, even when student teachers feel all is going well, the sheer experience of being observed is enough to cause them a high level of stress. This is in part enhanced because, as a student teacher, it is hard to be sure about how well you are doing, and you are also aware that the unpredictable nature of teaching means that any lesson has the potential to go seriously wrong.

Being assessed can cause stress

Dealing with disruptive behaviour

A second major source of stress is dealing successfully with pupils who misbehave. Student teachers can sometimes be overwhelmed by a feeling of panic when faced by an unruly class whom they feel they cannot control.

Some student teachers become worried about the brutalising effects on their personality of becoming strict disciplinarians. One student teacher, who was instructed by a teacher not to be so polite when giving instructions to the class, said:

but it feels uncomfortable. It feels like I am ordering people around. At the moment, I am battling with the fact that I have got to be more forceful at times, and I do not like that. I mean, I am being told by people that, basically, I have to lose my temper with certain people, and I find it very difficult to lose my temper.

It is not at all uncommon for student teachers to feel uncomfortable about having to be more assertive and to acquire a harder edge in the classroom.

Coping with a heavy workload

A third major source of stress involves coping with the general workload of being a teacher. Despite the fact that student teachers normally have a much reduced timetable (a half-timetable load is typical), students are faced with having to undertake many tasks and teaching topics for the first time. This means that planning and preparation, finding and developing curriculum materials, ensuring that they are knowledgeable about the subject matter, and conducting the necessary assessment of pupils' progress, including marking any written work, all takes much longer than it would for an experienced teacher. Indeed, the sheer intensity of the experience of being a student teacher, based on the physical demands it makes and the high level of uncertainty they face, can generate a high level of stress in student teachers. This is increased by the immense complexity of the thought processes that student teachers need to develop during teaching practice if they are to succeed. Student teachers are often puzzled by why problems occurred and how they should tackle them, which can lead to feelings of frustration and helplessness.

This sense of overload is increased by the fact that student teachers also face a whole host of contextual problems which result from teaching in a new school for a short period. These include the pressures resulting from having to get to know the teachers and pupils, where to find things, learning school procedures on a range of matters, and, for many student teachers, having to take new lodgings, make new travelling arrangements, and often live in isolation from existing friends and relations. As well as school-based concerns, the student teachers reported problems regarding weekend work, travelling, money, and getting home in the evening exhausted to the point of tearfulness.

Getting the teaching right

Another source of stress for student teachers is getting the teaching right in relation to the learning needs of their pupils. Student teachers often find it difficult to gauge the length of time that activities will last and whether they have pitched the work at the right level of difficulty. A particular problem can arise when pupils have not understood the work and the student teacher has no immediate idea of how to explain things differently or how to switch to an alternative activity that will more successfully lead to understanding. This sense of frustration is conveyed in the following comment:

> I have come away from one class thinking I have failed completely. The way it appeared to me that the lesson has gone, was that they had got nothing down on paper that I could see, and they had not understood what I had tried to get across to them.

Planning lessons

Planning lessons is often a cause of stress for student teachers. This is not surprising, as student teachers are teaching topics for the first time, and these may include topics they have not themselves previously studied. As a result, there are many frustrations that come from finding that you do not fully understand the topic yourself, not being able to find suitable materials to use, and not being sure about the key aspects of the topic that pupils need to learn. In addition, student teachers often worry about building up the work file of their lesson plans and schemes of work, which will be seen and assessed as part of the evaluation of their teaching practice. They often feel that the degree of planning and preparation has to be unrealistically detailed because it also has to serve this assessment purpose. One student teacher who found it difficult to create schemes of work because she was not getting enough guidance from teachers said:

> I am just worried that when [the university tutor] comes and she looks in my file, she is not going to find schemes of work when I have been doing my best to put them there.

Dealing with responsibilities

Becoming a teacher involves taking responsibilities. Failure to do your work well can have real and important consequences for pupils. For example, as a result of a pupil misbehaving in your lesson, the pupil's parents might be asked to come to the school to consider whether the pupil should be excluded; another example might be that you find after a lesson that you have explained something incorrectly just before pupils are due to take a test on the topic covered. There is a whole variety of situations that can occur in which student teachers can feel very concerned, rightly or wrongly, that what they have done has in some way led to pupils having a problem that could have been avoided. Similarly, there are situations where you may feel you have created problems for teachers in the school. If something serious goes wrong in this way, this can generate a very high level of stress. For many student teachers, their period of teaching practice may be the first time in their lives when they feel that what they are doing can have a serious impact on others in this way.

Not being regarded as a real teacher

Another common source of stress amongst student teachers is the perception that they are not being regarded by staff at the school as a 'real' teacher. Four factors are often identified in contributing to this feeling.

1 Periods of passive classroom observation when the 'real' teacher was 'demonstrating' their professional skills (such as teaching or taking the register).
2 Being given an incidental role in a classroom (e.g. helping individual pupils during a lesson) while the 'real' teacher took the lead. This generally gave rise to anxieties about being perceived by pupils as the 'teacher's little helper' – to quote one student teacher.
3 Uncertainty about whether to imitate the behaviours of the 'real' teachers (e.g. style of teaching, layout of classroom), when their classes were taken over by the student teacher.
4 When a teacher 'steals the show'; for example, one student teacher felt very upset by the way in which a teacher who was supposed to be observing the lesson kept interrupting, and put the point thus:

> The class are not going to listen to me if she [the teacher] keeps on chipping in, because it means that my authority is completely undermined.

Modifying your ideals and self-image

During teaching practice, student teachers also have to face the problem of the numerous self-doubts to which they are exposed.

Have they made the wrong career move? Will they be able to cope with the demands of the job? What will they do if they fail to qualify or decide teaching is not for them?

All student teachers start their teacher training course with certain ideals about how they want to teach and relate to pupils, which contribute to their image of themselves as a teacher. During their teaching practice they will inevitably find that certain ideals and aspects of their self-image need to be modified by their experience of what teaching is really like. Many student teachers will consequently experience periods of disillusionment during their teaching practice. For some student teachers this can be very painful, and indeed some will withdraw from a training course in part because they are unwilling or find it too difficult to modify their ideals and self-image.

For many student teachers, a major objective of teaching practice is simply to survive and qualify as a teacher. Indeed, the pressure on student teachers to cope with the demands of teaching practice can sometimes act as a barrier to their development, because it focuses their attention on the need to cope with immediate demands, rather than how to develop the understanding and skills needed for their professional development. Indeed, for some student teachers, the overwhelming nature of their fear of failure and sense of vulnerability makes them reluctant to look back at their work with a critical eye because it feels safer and more secure not to do so. If student teachers can be helped to develop effective coping strategies to deal with stress, this will greatly enhance their ability to improve the quality of their teaching as a whole.

Getting on with school staff

As a student teacher you have to get on as well as you can with other members of staff in the school, some of whom will need to give critical feedback on your work and to offer helpful advice and guidance on how you can do things better. You may find at times that receiving such advice is painful, and you may find that the chemistry of your relationship with the teachers directly involved with you in this way is not working well. For student teachers who are having problems during their teaching practice, it is sometimes hard to sustain a friendly relationship with these teachers. It can be particularly frustrating if you feel the advice you are getting is contradictory, unrealistic, or is not being adhered to by the teacher who is giving the advice. One student teacher was very upset about what he felt to be unrealistic expectations of him by teachers, and commented:

> if I sat in their lessons, I am sure I could come up with things they are not doing especially well, and yet ours have to be something out of this world.

From time to time such feelings may well occur, and when they come on a day in which you feel things are not going well, these are likely to increase the level of stress you experience. It is extremely important as a student teacher to maintain positive relationships with teachers in the school and not to take criticism personally. This will help you to build on the advice given rather than find yourself becoming defensive and entrenched in your own viewpoint.

Teaching about sensitive issues

How to handle the teaching of sensitive issues is also reported by some student teachers as a source of stress. Many student teachers are required to teach topics within the school's personal and social education programme, and this can include sensitive issues on areas in which the student teacher has limited knowledge. The problem is essentially one of knowing what to teach and how to present it, and being able to cope with the agitated responses of pupils who are clearly perturbed about the issues. Indeed, some pupils may refuse to discuss the topic and this can be very difficult for the student teacher to deal with. For example, one student teacher, referring to a social education lesson on divorce in a class where many children had divorced parents, said:

> they [the children] played clapping games for the second half of the lesson because they just did not want to do the work, and I was not going to be the one to say, 'You are going to learn about divorce and how it affects children'.

Finally, it is clear from studies of the concerns expressed by newly qualified teachers that many of the sources of stress facing student teachers during teaching practice, such as dealing with disruptive behaviour, coping with a heavy workload, evaluative feedback from their mentor, continue into the first year of teaching (e.g. Cains and Brown, 1998).

Identifying your sources of stress

Now list the sources of stress which you feel generate the most stress for you by completing Table 2.1. For the purpose of this exercise, I suggest you limit your list to ten, and put them in order, starting with the greatest source of stress. We will come back to your list later when we consider what action you can take to reduce your stress.

Table 2.1 Your top ten sources of stress

Do this!

1 _____

2 _____

3 _____

4 _____

5 _____

6 _____

7 _____

8 _____

9 _____

10 _____

3 Pre-empting stress

A number of studies have been published over the years which have looked at aspects of how teachers and other professionals can effectively deal with stress at work. A particularly interesting study of job burnout was that conducted by Cherniss (1995), which was mainly based on interviews of 26 'helping' professionals (seven high school teachers, seven mental health professionals, six public health nurses and six lawyers). All had just completed their professional training and were interviewed in their first year of practice. Cherniss then followed these subjects up some ten years later. The findings of this study contain a number of surprises, particularly in relation to exploring why some of those who had clearly experienced immense difficulties in their first year of practice went on to establish themselves as successful professionals in their chosen career, whilst some others who appeared to have made a positive start in the first year soon left their profession either disaffected or feeling unable to deal with the demands of the work.

Cherniss characterises burnout largely in terms of a loss of commitment and idealism concerning one's work caused by the experience of the stresses and frustrations of the work. The main sources of stress experienced by the subjects which appear to have precipitated early burnout involved worries about their own professional competencies, the constraints of working within a organisational system with its bureaucratic hassles, difficulties with clients, adjusting to boredom and routine, and a lack of collegiality. The most important factor in pre-empting burnout in the subjects appeared to be working in an environment that was supportive and that offered them a degree of autonomy in their working practices.

Cherniss reports that one of the key factors in those who developed into successful professionals was maintaining a good balance between home and work. These individuals neither just worked to live, nor just lived to work. Rather they maintained a good balance between having a healthy commitment to their professional lives and a healthy life outside work. Another interesting finding was that those successful in overcoming burnout seemed to have developed early insights into their careers, which enabled them to identify what type of work situations they found enjoyable and successful. They also had good negotiating skills, which enabled them to resolve organisational conflicts. Some had also experienced and overcome challenges in their lives before beginning their professional work, and this appeared to have given them greater resilience in overcoming initial setbacks.

Collegiality pre-empts stress

Cherniss also looked closely at five subjects (which included two of the teachers) who appeared to have recovered from problems in their first year of practice. In four cases these individuals had managed to change some aspect of their professional work, which enabled them to overcome their initial problems. Another important factor seems to have been the ability to develop a special interest in some aspect of their work from which they could gain satisfaction.

Those individuals who became successful professionals seem in large measure to have adjusted to professional life by developing more modest goals in relation to what they expected from work and what they felt they could realistically achieve. This involved an acceptance to some degree of a loss in the extent to which they felt their work could give their life 'meaning'. Cherniss outlines some implications relating to how burnout in the helping professions can be reduced. This includes giving professionals a greater role in the planning of change and more career counselling.

Studies of this type, which involve a follow-up, are very difficult to carry out, but they often do provide insights which can challenge our assumptions. One of the most interesting aspects of studying teachers' working lives is trying to explore how attitudes, behaviour and perceptions change over time. This type of data is particularly valuable in exploring the phenomena of burnout, where changes in the individuals and their circumstances can radically change how they approach and cope with their work.

On the basis of the findings of such studies, together with evaluations of the impact of in-service workshops designed to help teachers to manage stress, we now have a clear idea of which stress-management strategies are the most effective (Dunham and Varma, 1998; Mills, 1995; Rogers, 1992). However, one point that consistently comes through in the field of stress management is that 'prevention is better than cure'. The more you can do to minimise the sources of stress facing you, the better.

As we have seen in the last chapter, there are many potential sources of stress facing you, but they will only become actual sources of stress if you feel you are unable to deal with the situations successfully. There is much you can do to ensure that many potentially stressful situations do not arise in the first place. Such pre-emptive strategies fall into five main categories:

- time management
- being assertive
- organisational skills
- physical health
- mental health.

These are discussed below.

In addition, when stressful situations do occur, there are a range of coping actions you can take that will minimise the duration of the stress. Coping strategies will be the subject of the next two chapters.

Time management

The single most important thing a teacher can do to minimise sources of stress is to develop good time-management skills. The essence of a teacher's work involves getting a whole series of tasks completed on time and at an acceptable level of quality. There are few jobs that can compare with teaching for the variety of demands you have to deal with: lesson planning, classroom teaching, marking, administration, dealing with pupils' personal problems, school-based decision making, setting examinations, meeting parents, collaborating with colleagues, carrying out managerial responsibilities, helping new members of staff and student teachers, and the purchase of resources and equipment, such as textbooks, machinery and materials.

Time management is essential

Certainly anyone who has poor time-management skills will probably not even get to the first rung of qualifying as a teacher. Adequate time-management skills are essential for all teachers. Being able to cope with the demands of the job efficiently and effectively will have a bearing, directly or indirectly, on the quality of teaching and learning that takes place in your lessons. Almost all newly qualified teachers and most experienced teachers can further develop their time-management strategies to enable them to use their time to better effect.

Consequently you need to develop and enhance the skills that enable you to manage your time and effort to best effect. In addition, because of the changing nature of your work as a teacher as a result of your own career development and changes in teaching generally, you need to review and reflect regularly upon how well you are doing this.

Perhaps the essence of good time-management skills is the ability to prioritise your time so that the most important tasks and those tasks that have nearby deadlines are met first. This requires conscious planning. There are three real enemies to good time management. The first is simply doing tasks either in the order that they appear or in the order that suits you best (or a combination of these) rather than in the order that meets the demands facing you in the most effective way. The second enemy is allowing yourself to spend your time on tasks at a pace that feels right, with the danger that you spend more time on the tasks you are enjoying and less time on a task you want to avoid, regardless of which are the most important. The third enemy is procrastination.

You therefore need to think about how much time you spend on particular tasks, and decide whether your current practice needs to be altered. For example, you may be spending too much time planning lessons to the detriment of getting marking done on time.

Successful time management involves a number of important elements:

- Be aware of your time.
- Prioritise.
- Plan your time.
- Match time to tasks.
- Deal with small tasks quickly.
- Do not procrastinate.
- Be realistic.
- Be able to say 'no'.
- Delegate.

Be aware of your time

You need to think about how much time you spend on particular demands, and decide whether this needs to be altered. For example, you may be spending too much time planning and preparing lessons to the point where you are 'gilding the lily'. Analysis may reveal that you could reduce planning time without any noticeable loss of quality You may also be able to improve on the efficiency of your planning by, for example, making greater use of lesson plans given previously or by planning a course of lessons at the same time rather than individually.

Prioritise

You have to decide in which order to undertake various tasks, taking account of their importance and urgency. The more important a task is, the more you should budget time to carry it out well in advance of the deadline, so that you do not have to do a rushed job under pressure at the last minute. If the task is urgent, you need to be flexible in postponing another task that can wait. In general, you should loosely try to meet demands in the order they confront you, but be able to prioritise urgent and important tasks, as and when necessary.

Plan your time

You need to think about planning your time in the short term (the school day), the medium term (the school week) and the long term (the academic term and year). Your planning for each time frame ought to reflect your prioritising, so that by the end of each period the tasks with highest priority have been completed effectively, and those with lowest priority have been slotted in as and when appropriate. Advance planning is helpful in enabling you to prepare in good time and make necessary arrangements or take on other commitments in the light of such planning.

Match time to tasks

Everyone has preferences about when and how they work most efficiently for given tasks. For example, some teachers may find marking work late during a weekday evening is particularly productive, whilst others may find that using some time immediately after the end of a school day works better. Organising your time so that you can undertake particular tasks at your most efficient time for each can help you develop regular routines that work well.

Deal with small tasks quickly

There are a number of tasks that can be dealt with in a short period of time, either immediately or at an early opportunity. Getting such tasks done and out of the way as soon as possible helps to keep your desk clear. Leaving them for later often results in your finding that you have several rather small tasks needing to be done that begin to clutter up your planning, and their delay in completion may start to cause inconvenience to yourself and others. However, be alert to the fact that some such tasks, although small, may require more considered and careful attention, which you may need to think through or consult others about before acting.

Do not procrastinate

Once you have recognised that there is a task to be done, try to plan when you are going to carry it out, and then do so at that time. Much time can be wasted by thinking about starting a task on several occasions and each time deciding to leave it for no good reason, or because it involves some unpleasantness that you are inclined to put off.

Be realistic

You need to set yourself realistic demands, which means deciding what quality of work you can achieve in the time available. You may be trying to achieve a much higher quality than is really required, or carrying out a task much sooner than is sensible. Try not to accept unrealistic deadlines from others, as often such deadlines can easily be made more realistic.

Be able to say 'no'

Some teachers always say 'yes' when asked to undertake various tasks, and this can easily result in their becoming overloaded, and being the first to be approached when a new task needs to be allocated. Saying 'no', occasionally, provides others with feedback as to how busy you may be and whether you feel the task is something you could usefully take on at the moment (this will help others in the school decide how best to manage the allocation of tasks to staff as a whole).

Delegate

There are many tasks you can appropriately ask a colleague or a pupil to undertake and, from time to time, you should review whether some of the tasks you carry out should be delegated. You could easily find yourself, for example, spending a whole day, off and on, trying to find out something about a pupil's circumstances that a colleague was better placed to have found out in just a few minutes. You may also be spending too much time on routine tasks, such as handing out books, equipment, worksheets, collecting marks and checking progress, which could be better done by asking pupils to carry out some of these tasks.

However, you must take care not to become a time-obsessed tyrant. A good teacher should always be prepared to spend time talking to pupils and colleagues in a friendly manner and showing concern when problems arise. There is nothing worse than dealing with someone who places so much value on using their time to pursue their own personal agenda that they never seem to have time for others. In fact, it is good time-management skills that enable you to have the space to sustain healthy relationships with others.

As well as developing time-management skills yourself, you should be helping others to do so. For example, you should help pupils become aware of how to organise and pace their efforts in meeting deadlines within a lesson or over a longer period. In your dealings with colleagues, you can also help them to plan how tasks which affect you and others need to be organised so that appropriate deadlines and task allocations are set: for example, planning that pupils do not have too many coursework deadlines falling on the same date, or that time to mark examination work does not coincide unnecessarily with other busy periods in the school.

Time-management skills are not a panacea that will alleviate all time pressures on you. Nevertheless, they are a major factor in keeping avoidable pressures to a minimum, and helping you to maintain a high level of efficiency in undertaking the variety of tasks facing you. Indeed, they are one of the important sets of skills that new teachers need to develop in the early years of teaching, and then need to develop further as their role and commitments in school alter.

Being assertive

Being assertive is another important skill that all teachers need to develop. Being assertive means being able to communicate your wishes and feelings to others so that they can be taken into account when decisions are being made or when the other person is considering their behaviour (see box). Assertiveness is best considered as falling midway between aggressiveness and compliance. An aggressive person takes the stance that they want to get what they want, and are unwilling to compromise. A compliant person is someone who readily agrees to go along with other people's wishes whether it suits them or not.

The assertive teacher

Assertive teachers view their own needs and wants as equal to those of others. They are honest and respectful in their dealings with others and try to work towards a mutually beneficial outcome of the situation in hand.

The problem with aggressive people is that they are unable to form a sound working relationship with colleagues or pupils, in large part because they are not prepared to consider other people's points of view or needs, and may often, as a result, end up taking action which backfires on themselves.

At the other extreme, compliant people tend to say yes to colleagues too often, and easily end up taking on too many tasks (because people often first approach those who tend to say yes) or doing tasks in a way they disagree with. Such people also run into problems in their dealings with pupils, because they do not make their demands or expectations clear and lack firmness, and as a result often appear to be inconsistent. Both aggressive teachers and compliant teachers can generate stress for themselves through their own behaviour.

The assertive teacher is a teacher who is able to express their point of view clearly, and who seeks to establish a sound working relationship with colleagues and pupils that is in their mutual interest. Such a stance often builds up goodwill, and others will feel that they are able to have trust in their dealings with you.

Assertiveness is a social skill. The essence of assertiveness is being honest and respectful in your dealings with others. Whilst some people seem to have developed this social skill early in their lives, others only come to realise that they still need to develop this skill as a result of the problems that they find they generate at work for themselves and others by being either aggressive or compliant. Unfortunately, some individuals who are generally compliant try to be assertive by being aggressive from time to time, because they mistakenly view assertiveness as meaning that you get your own way in the form of an 'I win – You lose' outcome. In fact, the assertive person is simply someone who tries to act in a collegial manner, who is seeking a 'win–win' outcome, and who is able to make their own views and needs clear in the process.

Assertiveness lies mid-way between aggression and compliance

A very interesting study was reported by Bowers (1995), who looked at the effectiveness of the approaches used by teachers to deal with problems and conflicts in terms of their assertiveness. The study compared the stress levels of teachers who were categorised as adopting one of four conflict management styles:

- those who tended to adopt an aggressive/confrontive style (controlling people and situations and seeking to dominate them)
- those who used an avoidant/reactive style (passivity, withdrawing from threat, avoiding confrontation)

- those who used an observant/introspective style (observing and analysing oneself and others, and adopting a listening and counselling mode of behaviour)
- those who used an assertive/persuasive style (standing up for oneself without being 'pushy', and willingness to collaborate).

He found that teachers with an aggressive/confrontive style seemed to experience the most stress. Such teachers may achieve some control over their environment by being aggressive, but it was at the cost of experiencing a relatively higher level of stress.

Teachers using the avoidant/reactive style appeared to see their problems as somewhat intractable and had now come to adopt a strategy of ignoring or denying the existence of the problems. Whilst this offered some protection, there was still an emotional cost involved in trying to sustain this sense of mental distance while accommodating to a situation where the problems in reality continue to exist.

Teachers with an observant/introspective style came next in terms of their level of stress. Broadly speaking, this style gave teachers a degree of emotional control over their experience of stress by focusing on their own motives and feelings in responding to a stress-inducing situation.

The teachers who adopted an assertive/persuasive style experienced the least stress. Bowers argues that assertiveness may contribute to effective coping in two ways. First, you are able to express your belief in your rights in ways that do not override or negate the rights of others. Second, you are able to argue logically and simply for your point of view without resorting, on the one hand, to coercion or, on the other hand, to physical withdrawal. As a result, assertiveness enables you to apply your intellect to resolve problems and thereby to retain more control over your actions. This will, in most stress-inducing situations, provide the most successful strategy of dealing with problems and pre-empting the occurrence of stress.

Lloyd (1995) has outlined a number of important aspects to being assertive and the need to develop the skills involved in resolving conflicts and problems by influencing, listening and negotiating so that others choose to cooperate willingly. Assertive behaviour leads to success without retaliation and encourages open and honest relationships.

Choose your words carefully

One important aspect of being assertive is to be able to communicate your view to others in a way that neither offends (being aggressive) nor is self-deprecating (compliant). For example, suppose you are asked by a colleague to do something you do not wish to do. Here are some possible ways of expressing your view:

- *'You must be kidding – that sounds ridiculous to me.'* This is aggressive, accusatory, and invites defensiveness.
- *'Sorry, I'm tied up doing something else then.'* This is the type of statement that a compliant person will often use to avoid agreeing to do something; it is essentially dishonest, and avoids having to say 'no', which a compliant person finds difficult to do.
- *'No thanks. I appreciate you asking me, but it's not really my type of thing.'* This is assertive – it is honest and appreciative.
- *'Is there some other way I can help out?'* This is compliant – in order to avoid saying no, the compliant person sometimes ends up agreeing to do something else instead which could be worse that what they were asked to do in the first place.
- *'I can't believe you've asked me that when I am so busy with other things.'* This is aggressive, blameful and invites defensiveness.
- *'Sorry, I would have been happy to help at another time but I have just got too much on my plate over the next couple of weeks.'* This is assertive, honest and tactful.

Lloyd also highlights the way in which assertive behaviour involves using certain types of words, as is illustrated by comparing the following statements.

Use 'I-statements' rather than 'you-statements'

'I would like to finish this point' (assertive) is better than *'You are always interrupting me'* (aggressive).

Use factual descriptions rather than judgements

'Your marking was two days late. If it happens again with the next set of scripts it will create a lot of problems getting the reports done on time. I really need you to meet our agreed deadlines' (assertive) is better than *'If you don't change your attitude you are going to be in real trouble'* (aggressive).

Express feelings and opinions fairly and declare ownership of them

'I really think we need to revise the school prospectus now' (assertive – a clear and personal view expressed) is better than *'Everyone knows the school prospectus is a disgrace'* (aggressive – states opinion as fact, denies personal ownership of the opinion, controlling).

Use clear directives and requests rather than be indirect, hint or presume

'Could you please take this to the school office?' (assertive – a clear and unambiguous request – requiring a clear response) is better than *'Are you thinking of taking this to the school office?'* (indirect – other person not sure whether this is a request to do this, or whether you are just checking, or whether you feel they should already have done this).

Convey assertive body language

Lloyd has highlighted some of the differences in the body language of those who are aggressive, assertive and compliant, in terms of their posture, gestures, facial expressions and voice. These differences are illustrated in Table 3.1.

Table 3.1 Aggressive, assertive and compliant body language

Aggressive body language	Assertive body language	Compliant body language
Posture is tense and rigid; movements are jerky	Posture is erect and relaxed; movements are smooth	Posture is slumped; shoulders bend forward, shifting down
Gestures with clenched hands; points, nods sharply	Gestures with open hands; movements are casual	Gestures are nervous; frequent nods of head and twists of body
Facial expression is characterised by furrowed brow and tight lips; displays displeasure by scowl and flushed face	Facial expression is characterised by genuine smiles and relaxed mouth; displays displeasure by serious eye contact	Facial expression is characterised by wide-eyes, rapid blinking and nervous smiles; shows displeasure with averted eyes and a guilty look
Voice is harsh and precise; makes statements sound like orders	Voice is pleasant, relaxed and even-flowing	Voice is quiet and high pitched, with 'uhm' and 'ah' hesitations

Four steps to assertive communication

Lloyd also highlights four steps by which you can increase the power of your communication whilst remaining assertive and not resorting to aggressive behaviour. These are:

1 Repeat

This is the basic level of assertiveness and simply involves you in repeating the original request. For example, *'Can you please tell me how I can contact Mr Green?'* By repeating a statement or question, coupled with a firm tone of voice and eye contact, you will increase the power of your request.

2 Command

If the person you are talking to continues to ignore the request or refuses to cooperate, you should change your request to a command. For example, *'Please tell me how I can contact Mr Green.'* Command statements convey more power than a request but are still regarded as polite.

3 Add emotion

The next level of power is to add emotion to your statement through your tone of voice and/or explicitly referring to your feelings. For example, *'I am getting annoyed by this, please tell me how I can contact Mr Green.'*

4 Introduce consequences

Finally, you can increase the level of power further by introducing consequences. Consequences are not threats, they are simply statements of what you intend to do (or what will happen) if you do not get the cooperation you have asked for. Stating the consequences gives the other person a further chance to change their behaviour and cooperate. The consequences need to be believable and you must be prepared to carry out the action you have outlined. For example, *'If you do not tell me how to contact Mr Green, I shall telephone him at his home number tonight and point out that you refused to allow me to contact him during the afternoon.'* Sometimes, consequences will follow without your taking any action, and pointing these out will be powerful enough. For example, *'If I don't contact Mr Green this afternoon, he will end up making an expensive mistake which the school is going to have to pay for.'*

It is interesting to note that the underlying strategy involved in these four steps has been used by some writers to outline how teachers can increase the power of their communications when exerting discipline in the classroom. Indeed, Rogers (1992) explicitly builds this into his notion of how to make an effective discipline plan that enables you to increase the power of your communications when pupils do not cooperate. Rogers points out how such an approach can help you to avoid losing your temper in a situation where a pupil is blatantly defiant. Rogers refers to this approach as enabling the teacher to be decisive by keeping the pupils' attention focused on the behaviour which you are asking them to engage in (e.g. getting on with their work) and not being side-tracked into a disciplinary confrontation which can be provoked if the pupil says something like *'Why are you always picking on me?'* One such technique, which Rogers refers to as 'blocking', involves the teacher simply repeating a clear directive over and over again (e.g. *'Sit up properly and get on with your work'*) and ignoring what the pupil says in response until the pupil eventually complies.

Organisational skills

Sound organisational skills, such as those listed below, can also do much to pre-empt unnecessary sources of stress.

- Plan and prepare carefully.
- Anticipate problems.
- Develop effective routines to deal with tasks.
- Make notes on what needs to be done.

For example, during classroom teaching you will have a great number of decisions to make to maintain a steady and coherent flow to the lesson. Good planning and preparation in advance of the lesson can save valuable thinking time, which you can then use during the lesson itself to deal with the decisions that need to be made. For example, in your lesson notes you may have a list of the correct answers to some of the questions you are going to ask; you can ensure that materials that will be needed are ready to hand; you decide in advance how much time is needed for the different learning activities.

Similarly, outside the classroom, the more organised you are in your work, the less pressure you will put yourself under. Once you have established effective routines to deal with your workload, you will also feel more confident that when new tasks appear, you will be able to deal with them. Being disorganised can lead to stress in two ways. First, being disorganised means that you are more likely to find yourself in difficult situations that directly generate stress. Second, being disorganised undermines your sense of control over events, and thereby makes you more vulnerable to experiencing stress each time a new demand occurs.

When you are engaged in organisational tasks involving colleagues, always make sure that you check with them what needs to be done. It is also important to consult colleagues over your ideas, as most people will resent important decisions being made which affect them if they feel they were not consulted. Schools very much depend on establishing a collegial atmosphere amongst staff. No matter how enthusiastic and certain you feel about your ideas, it is essential to sound colleagues out before you attempt to put any plans into action. A great deal of stress can be generated for yourself and your colleagues if conflicts and dissension arise from an over-zealous approach on your part to school management decision making.

Plan and prepare carefully

Much of the stress experienced by teachers stems from the sheer volume and pace of decision making they have to sustain throughout a school day. The more you can do in advance to reduce the need for later mental effort the better. For example, having to hand a list of answers to questions that you intend to set as an exercise to be completed by pupils during a lesson means that as you circulate around the room checking on pupils' progress and helping pupils having difficulties with their work, you will not have to waste valuable time by working out answers yourself during the lesson. Similarly, time spent rehearsing the use of equipment or procedures prior to using them in a lesson means that you can remain much more relaxed when they are used in your teaching.

Anticipate problems

One of the characteristics that seems to distinguish teachers who are able to pre-empt stress is their ability to anticipate problems. For example, if you know that at a meeting you are due to have with colleagues there is a strong likelihood that one of your colleagues may raise an issue that will generate acrimonious debate, you can to some extent deal with that in advance by having a conversation with the colleague in the hope that the issue can be resolved to that teacher's satisfaction without its needing to be aired at the meeting.

Similarly, if you know that certain pupils have a tendency to react to coercion in a hostile manner, you can try to ensure that your approach to teaching them enables you to deal with difficulties they encounter at an early stage or that you use a form of encouragement to motivate them that they do not experience as coercion.

Anticipating problems can also be linked to those sources of stress which you know you are particularly prone to. For example, if you know that you become easily upset when you are running behind with your marking, you can pre-empt this by getting the pupils to do some marking of each other's work in the last part of a lesson, so that particular group of pupils' work will not need to be marked that evening when you are already aware that some examination scripts will have to be marked.

Develop effective routines to deal with tasks

You can pre-empt much stress by having efficient and effective routines to deal with certain tasks. This reduces stress by enabling you to operate without having to spend time thinking afresh about when and how you are going to tackle these tasks each time they arise. For example, you may be involved in a system of recording pupils' progress in a certain way on a three-weekly basis. Each time the end of the three-week period comes, you might find yourself needing to collate marks, or collect in pupils' work, or carry out some other activity that is needed to complete this task. However, you might find that by keeping a running log of progress each time work is marked, the final recording session may become no more than a semi-automatic transmission of data you already have to hand. Building in routines of this sort can often mean that a task which could become a regularly occurring unpleasant and aggravating chore could instead be one carried out by you efficiently and effectively with almost minimal awareness on your part.

Another example might be that you are worried about whether you have kept colleagues informed of special medication that one of the pupils in your form is required to take from time to time when the need arises. As a result, you may find yourself waking up in a cold sweat mentally rehearsing whether you have done this properly. Again, introducing a simple procedure on your part of keeping a diary where you record all such special medication, and where you sign each fortnight a note to yourself that you have passed this information on to appropriate colleagues, means that you can rest assured that you have discharged this responsibility as required. This is not to say that for every possible task you need such routines. However, for those tasks where you feel that you are experiencing a great deal of stress that could be pre-empted in this way, then making the effort to organise such routines will be well worthwhile.

Make notes on what needs to be done

Making notes of what needs to be done is one of the commonest and most effective ways to pre-empt stress. Many people will experience intense stress when they start to hold in their mind a list of important tasks that need to be completed. Indeed, being interrupted at a time when you are mentally rehearsing such a list to yourself can be very frustrating. Some teachers use up a lot of mental effort by trying to remember what they have to do, and also worrying about whether there is something really important that they have overlooked or forgotten. Making lists can be helpful both in reducing the mental effort of memorising and in providing you with items that you can tick off as and when tasks are done. Such lists can also help you to prioritise tasks and ensure you have carried out precursor activities, such as checking something with a colleague during the lunch break that will then enable you to carry out a certain task during the afternoon.

Physical health

Teaching is a physically demanding job. You will be standing for long periods of time, you will be rushing from place to place in the school, and you will occasionally be carrying heavy loads. Being physically healthy will clearly help you cope with such demands.

There are three aspects of doing your work that require particular attention:

- voice care
- body posture
- keeping fit.

Voice care

It is essential that you look after your voice. You need to think carefully about how you project your voice so that you can be heard clearly, but do not strain your vocal chords. You should avoid shouting at pupils. You also need to think carefully about your breathing pattern. The experience of stress is an emotional response to the perception of threat. You will be more likely to feel your situation is threatening if you can sense that your body is straining to meet the demands on it, and that you are getting increasingly uncomfortable as problems arise. Any feeling that you are straining your voice can contribute to a sense of anxiety. Taking care of your voice will make you feel much more comfortable in your teaching.

The following checklist is typical of those used in workshops with teachers looking at aspects of voice care:

- Try to relax your throat area.
- Always breathe from your diaphragm.
- Make sure you take in enough air.
- Avoid straining your voice (especially if you have a cold).
- Avoid shouting.
- Do not talk over class noise.
- Project your voice to the back wall.
- Do not smoke.
- Do not drink alcohol if you have a sore throat.
- Avoid chalk dust.

It is very important to learn how to use your voice properly in the first place, to breathe properly, to develop the pitch in your voice that is most natural, and to project your voice without strain. If you feel your voice is suffering, you must try and rest it as much as possible, and avoid taking on any extra demands that will put it under additional pressure.

Body posture

Similarly, teachers can sometimes develop bad posture habits. Instead of standing erect with a straight back, they may stand more slouched, with their head bent slightly forward, which places more strain on their back and neck muscles. Inevitably, this will lead to a greater feeling of tension, so that when a problem arises the teacher may already be feeling tense and may be disposed to assume that the problem, rather than their poor posture, is the cause of this feeling of tension.

Keeping fit

Feeling tired can exacerbate feelings of stress. If you are already feeling tired because you are unfit physically, this will make you more vulnerable to stress at work. Two things you can try to do are to avoid getting overweight and to avoid smoking.

In addition, taking regular walks at weekends or engaging in some type of sports activity, such as swimming or badminton, will help keep your body in good shape for the demands and rigours of the school day.

Keeping fit builds up your energy levels

Building up your energy levels by taking regular exercise can also markedly increase your ability to deal effectively with stress. Doing so, however, involves you in making a real commitment to taking exercise, and to maintain this once you have started. This can sometimes be difficult, in part because it involves time and expense, and in part because when you are tired, taking exercise can appear to be counter-intuitive. However, the benefits will be significant, and once it begins to pay off in reducing stress at work, you will find that you become more efficient at dealing with demands at work, and this will lead to your having more time and energy to continue with such exercise. In effect, it creates a virtuous circle, in that each benefit you gain will in turn create a further benefit.

Mental health

Your state of mental health has an important influence on how you view your situation and whether stress will be generated. Staying positive and feeling mentally healthy can do much to pre-empt the occurrence of stress. The following three factors are particularly important:

- a well-balanced personality
- a positive attitude towards solving problems
- high ego-strength.

A well-balanced personality

As noted in chapter 1, a well-balanced and secure personality can help minimise the level of stress teachers will experience at work. Although you cannot easily change your personality, you can make an effort to develop more positive attitudes towards dealing with problems. Having a cynical or negative stance towards the world means that you are much more likely to perceive situations as threatening.

A positive attitude towards solving problems

Individuals who have a positive attitude towards solving problems are able to deal with the challenges they face in a more efficient and productive manner. Such individuals typically have a happy and secure home life and are likely to be less troubled by problems at work. It is thus important that you have interests outside of school, and do things in your personal life that you can look forward to and enjoy. A healthy balance between work at school and your life outside school can help contribute to a sense of mental health that will make you far less vulnerable to experiencing stress when problems arise at work. You are also far less likely to interpret problems at school as evidence of a personal failing on your part.

High ego-strength

Some researchers have used the term 'ego-strength' to refer to this type of self-assurance and self-confidence. In some ways ego-strength can be regarded as the opposite of the personality trait of neuroticism. A person high on neuroticism is easily upset, endlessly worries about problems, and is likely to regard difficulties as evidence of personal failings on their part. In contrast, someone high on ego-strength is much more stable and secure in dealing with demands made on them, is likely to face problems calmly and rationally, and will regard difficulties as evidence that the problem is not easy to deal with rather than something which reflects on them personally.

As already indicated, you cannot easily change your personality, but the point about ego-strength is that it highlights how a person's sense of security or vulnerability plays a part in triggering stress. Having a healthy home life and interests outside school enhances your ego-strength. We all know of people who often worry about things when they have not got anything else to think about, and who start to make mountains out of mole hills. Making sure you live a balanced life will help you develop a balanced personality.

Interestingly a similar point has been made by writers who have sought to link how a teacher ticks as a person to their behaviour as a teacher. Such writers have highlighted that the type of person who is able to feel secure and comfortable in dealing with difficult demands in school must first be secure and comfortable with themselves as a person.

Generally speaking, teachers as a professional group are quite healthy mentally. This is in part a reflection of the fact that to qualify successfully as a teacher you need to be selected for and complete a teacher training course which ensures that the vast majority of people whose personality characteristics would ill suit them for a career in teaching are not able to join the profession. Nevertheless, it is important to ensure that through the lifestyle you adopt you help enhance rather than undermine a well-balanced personality.

4 Direct-action coping strategies

Coping strategies are any action you can take to deal with stress at work. In this and the next chapter we will be looking at the coping actions which appear to be particularly effective. At the end of the next chapter you will be asked to consider how these can be used to deal with the ten sources of stress you listed at the end of chapter 1.

Common coping actions

Many studies have been conducted which have looked at the coping actions used by teachers. For example, in a survey by Cockburn (1996a, 1996b) of coping strategies used by primary teachers to deal with stress, the ten most effective strategies reported by the teachers were:

- Ensure that you understand the work you are about to teach.
- Prepare lessons thoroughly.
- Find the humour in the situation.
- Abandon sessions which are not going well.
- Discuss your concerns with other teachers in the school.
- Get to know your pupils as individuals.
- Set priorities.
- Make lists.
- Share your failures.
- Chat to colleagues about recreational interests, etc.

Similarly, in a survey by Benmansour (1998) of coping strategies used by secondary school teachers to deal with stress, the most frequently used strategies reported by the teachers were:

- Plan and organise lessons in advance.
- Adopt strategies and procedures to improve pupils' performance.
- Try to be more realistic and adapt to circumstances.
- Double your effort.
- Use more motivating teaching methods in the class.
- Get used to and adapt to problems.
- Talk about problems with colleagues or friends.
- Try not to exaggerate the importance of problems.
- Relax after work.
- Talk about problems during meetings.

In a study I conducted with primary school teachers, some teachers reported that having a strong religious faith helped them to cope with stress and work, and that praying and attending religious services were effective coping actions for them (Kyriacou and Pratt, 1985).

An analysis of these and other studies of coping actions used by teachers (Borg and Falzon, 1990; Pithers and Soden, 1998; Travers and Cooper, 1996) indicates that the coping actions teachers report using most frequently are those listed in the box below.

The top ten coping actions

Try to keep problems in perspective

Avoid confrontations

Try to relax after work

Take action to deal with problems

Keep your feelings under control

Devote more time to particular tasks

Discuss problems and express your feelings to others

Have a healthy home life

Plan ahead and prioritise

Recognise your own limitations

Try to keep problems in perspective

Perhaps the single most powerful coping strategy that a teacher can use is to keep problems in perspective. Indeed many people use the technique of contrasting an unpleasant situation or event with something much worse as a means of not getting upset, such as when people say after denting their car in a minor accident, 'Well no one got hurt, and that's the important thing.' This attempt to keep things in perspective is illustrated in the following comment:

I enjoy travelling, and I make sure that every summer we go abroad to somewhere exotic. I enjoy teaching, and I get on well with pupils and colleagues. When I do get up-tight about something I just think to myself that it's all part of life's rich tapestry and measured against the awful things that can happen in life there is no point allowing the problem to take on a significance it just doesn't deserve. When I first started teaching

I think I saw every issue as a matter of life and death – I have come a long way since then.

Avoid confrontations

Another very important way to minimise stress is to avoid confrontations. As teachers gain experience they become very adept at spotting the signs which signal that a problem may be developing.

The problem may stem from your dealings with pupils, such as when you can see that pupils are getting restless, bored, are having difficulties with the work, or are not as attentive as they should be. Immediate action can quickly restore a positive working climate to the lesson. However, one or more pupils may start to misbehave and you will then need to deal with this. In such a situation, it is important to be aware that there are four main scenarios that can precipitate a confrontation with a pupil.

- You make a sarcastic or disparaging remark to a pupil that they regard as immensely unjust, unfair, and an abuse of your position of authority. Pupils are particularly sensitive to comparisons being made with others, or being ridiculed or exposed to public embarrassment in any way.
- You suddenly become aggressive yourself, lose your temper, and start to shout at a pupil, or use any form of strong verbal or physical intimidation. An example of such intimidation would be to point aggressively and repeatedly at a pupil.
- A pupil is under pressure because they feel frustrated by the work, and being pressured by you to continue to do work that they just do not understand will expose their lack of understanding to you and their peers.
- A pupil feels under pressure because of circumstances outside the class such as problems with another teacher, other pupils, or in their life at home, which make them highly vulnerable to over-react to any additional pressure placed on them.

A confrontation with a pupil can develop in a split second, and before anyone realises it, you or the pupil may have said or done something they regret. It is thus extremely important for you to stay calm (or become calm) as soon as you are aware that a confrontation has developed. If you remain calm, then the pupil will also become calm. Being calm will also help you think more clearly and rationally about the best way to deal with the situation. In contrast, being angry will tend to narrow your thinking and close down your options of how to act, and may thereby lead you to make an immediate and unnecessary demand or ultimatum (e.g. *You either apologise to me now, or we go straight to the Head's office*).

You can quickly defuse a confrontation by staying calm, continuing the communication in a quiet voice in private (rather than loudly and in front of other pupils) and deferring further action, if appropriate, to the end of the lesson. A comment such as the following would be a good example of this approach: *'Just calm down. There is no need for anyone to get upset over things. I suggest we sort this out at the end of the lesson. For the time being, just try your best to do the work I've set or sit quietly without disturbing anyone else. I'll come back and check a few things with you a bit later. Okay?'*

One of the golden rules in dealing with a confrontation is not to place yourself in a position where the pupil must be seen to publicly back down or you will be seen to have lost authority. This is sometimes referred to as an 'I win – You lose' scenario. In fact you will earn the respect of the vast majority of pupils if you can display the social skills needed to quickly diffuse such confrontations in a fair and reasonable manner. Developing such skills will enable you to minimise any stress that could develop when a confrontation arises. This is illustrated in the following comment:

> Confrontations become much less frequent, of course, as experience grows. I increasingly interview an awkward child alone and often a discussion of problems helps attitude. In any case, the next lesson may be entirely different, for no obvious reason. I still over-react, however, since I expect what may be unreasonably high standards of behaviour.

Confrontations can also develop with colleagues. With experience, teachers again develop the skill of knowing how to interact with a colleague in a way that avoids a confrontation. Some of the points made about being assertive rather than aggressive outlined in the previous chapter are important here. As you get to know your colleagues well, you will be aware of what will annoy or upset one colleague rather than another. Some colleagues always like to be consulted about things in a tactful and respectful manner. Other colleagues may prefer you to be frank with them.

In addition, you need be sensitive about if, when and how certain issues need to be raised with a colleague. In many cases, problems may well be hypothetical or the event may have passed, and there is little to be served in raising an issue which may simply annoy or upset a colleague to no good purpose. To protect yourself from unnecessary stress, there are times when it makes sense for you to lie low if you feel a confrontation could be generated by your presence that will be avoided if you simply keep out of someone else's way for a couple of days.

Avoid confrontations

Try to relax after work

One of the main symptoms of stress is a feeling of tension. Anything you can do after work to help you relax will do much to dissipate the stress, and help you arrive at the beginning of the next school day refreshed and in a good mental and physical state. This is illustrated in the following comment:

> I keep my home life and school life separate, as far as possible nowadays, which I admit is not too easy. I work very hard at school and try to get as much done there as I can. When I'm home I just enjoy doing things with my family. I have learnt the importance of relaxing at home. When my children have gone to bed at night, I will do some marking or preparation work, but what I try very hard not to do is to short-change my family and myself by spending all evening doing school work.

The reference here to short-changing one's family is an important one. Stress at work can easily spill over into your home life. If as a result this begins to generate stress for you at home, you can get sucked into a vicious circle of stress at work and at home feeding into each other. It is absolutely essential that as far as possible you retain a healthy personal life so that you can fully relax when you are away from school on a regular basis.

Take action to deal with problems

As we will see later, when we look at direct-action strategies, it is often far easier to deal with problems when they first appear than to allow them to develop and then have to deal with them after they have started to cause you stress. With experience, teachers become adept at knowing which problems, if ignored, will eventually make matters much worse. Allowing pupils to be cheeky or unruly in their first few lessons with you at the start of a new school year will almost certainly lead to problems that will have to be dealt with later. Allowing newly introduced administrative routines to be largely ignored or followed incorrectly by colleagues will inevitably make it much harder to tighten them up later, and may even induce resentment when colleagues perceive this as another unnecessary change.

As a teacher you cannot deal with every possible problem at the outset. However, you do need to develop a sense of those problems that do require prioritising in this way. This is illustrated in the following comment:

> I always try to deal with problems as soon as they arise, otherwise some problems just grow and become too complex to deal with later.

What is also certainly the case is that if a problem is causing you stress, you cannot ignore it for long before you start to feel the effects of the stress generated. This is because ignoring a problem also requires a certain amount of energy, since part of your mind will naturally be trying to pay attention to the problem whilst at the same time another part of your mind is trying to stay focused on other tasks and activities. This state of affairs in itself will generate tension and feelings of mental exhaustion at the end of a school day.

Another aspect of dealing with problems is that it creates a positive attitude of mind on your part, in which you feel in control and able to deal with demands as and when they arise. Not dealing with problems creates a negative mental state, which can start to generate feelings of powerlessness that in turn make you feel more vulnerable to stress when new demands occur.

Keep your feelings under control

The experience of stress in the form of anger, frustration or depression can sometimes feel like an inevitable consequence of the situation you find yourself in. In fact, there is much you can do to reduce this emotional response or indeed to remove it altogether. First, you need to be aware of the way you respond to stressful situations. Some people have a strong predisposition to lose their temper when they are frustrated, whilst others tend to feel depressed. Such emotions can be effectively curtailed by two strategies. The first is to retain a sense of emotional control. You can prevent yourself getting angry or depressed by trying to relax and telling yourself to remain positive. The second strategy is to prevent yourself thinking about the situation in a manner that makes it seem worse and working yourself up into state of greater and greater emotion. These two palliative techniques will be dealt with in the next chapter. Staying relaxed is not always easy, as is illustrated in the next comment, but it can certainly do much to prevent minor sources of stress feeling like major ones.

> I have learned to relax (not react too much) to stressful times in the class-room – perhaps the strain of doing this is worse than reacting. I cannot use my hand as a quick discipline sanction so I find dealing with discipline very stressful.

This comment also reflects how stress can sometime be increased if you feel that the way in which you would like to deal with the situation is blocked in some way. In the above case, this teacher feels that he would like to react physically to pupil indiscipline, but as this is not allowable, he clearly feels frustrated that he has to deal with such situations in other ways. Wanting to respond physically to a stressful situation, by hitting someone, slamming a door or desk lid, shouting or swearing, may feel like a natural instinct to many people, but teachers know that such behaviour is simply not acceptable at school, so their efforts to deal with a stressful situation have to involve a great deal of emotional control over what may in some ways feel like a more spontaneous response.

Devote more time to particular tasks

As we saw in the last chapter, good time-management skills are crucial to managing the demands on you. However, the tasks facing you in teaching are such that even with the best time-management skills in play, you will never reach a point where all the demands made on you can be spread out evenly. There will inevitably be times when you have a much heavier load of work to carry out than at other times. At such times it is crucial to make sure that you devote enough time to complete the most important tasks in a satisfactory manner. Thus, for example, during periods when examination scripts need to be marked, you may well need to devote less time to planning lessons. Whilst you may be able to build in some extra time during particularly busy periods, you may need to accept that not everything you routinely do may be done that particular week. However, each person's strategy needs to suit them. This is illustrated in the following comment:

> I am the sort of person who only feels comfortable when I am on top of my work, so when I know there is a lot to do I just get on and do it until it's done, even if it takes all night.

This teacher finds that putting in additional time during busy periods seems to be the strategy that suits her best. In contrast, another teacher might try to rearrange their other commitments so that working late into the night can be avoided. In the latter case, the need for a good night's sleep may be more important than trying to get a backlog of work cleared quickly. The difference between these two teachers is in part a difference in personality concerning how they feel about getting tasks done.

Discuss problems and express your feelings to others

Sharing your problems and concerns with others can be helpful in two main ways:

- They may be able to offer advice, guidance and practical help to deal with the source of stress.
- They may be able to offer you emotional support by expressing sympathy and understanding for your situation.

In schools where there is a positive climate of mutual support amongst staff, it is far easier to share concerns with others and to receive social support when you are having problems. For reasons that are not fully understood, such social support seems to be a powerful factor in reducing a person's level of stress. It may be because it reduces the sense in which having a problem is regarded as a sign of personal failure, and hence not dealing successfully with a source of stress is perceived to be less threatening than it would be in another school where the level of social support was lower. The following comment illustrates how seeking support can precipitate useful advice and guidance from a colleague:

> I try not to worry – but calmly try to sort things out. I do discuss problems with my head of department and follow his advice if possible.

Have a healthy home life

All teachers need to maintain a good balance between their home life and their working life. Having a healthy home life can act as a major buffer to stress at work, in ways that have already been outlined. This sentiment is illustrated by the following comment:

> I talk about outside interests and hobbies, and never allow the job to dominate one's life. In other words, by action and thought make sure that one has more than one identity.

This comment makes particular mention of the way in which a healthy home life can strengthen your sense of personal identity and self-worth, thereby making you less likely to ruminate for long periods about problems arising at work.

Have a good home life

Plan ahead and prioritise

Sound planning and preparation enables you to avoid the panic that can occur when at the last minute you find you have too many tasks to deal with that require urgent attention. The following comment illustrates the importance of also being able to accept that you have done your best in the time available.

> I am well organised – you have to be – and I use lists to check that what needs to be done is done. It's impossible to do everything perfectly, so I have learnt to accept that I have done what needs to be done as well as I can in the time available, and then I get on with the next task.

Teachers frequently receive advice and guidance regarding their performance. This can be given during in-service workshops provided by outside experts, or it may appear in Ofsted handbooks and reports, in books about improving your classroom practice, or in public pronouncements. One criticism often made about such advice is that the level of performance advocated is often far above what can realistically be achieved in the time that teachers have available to them. Whilst aiming for 'best possible practice' is a noble objective, teachers have to carry out a whole range of tasks. A teacher whose classroom teaching is excellent, but whose marking of pupils' work is superficial, will not have achieved the right balance. It is therefore a good idea to have a sense of what it means to carry out a task at a level that is 'good enough'. You need to carry out as many tasks as possible at the good enough level. If some tasks are below this level, you need to prioritise their improvement. The corollary of this is that you also need to be able to accept that some tasks are carried out at the good enough level which, if more time was available, could be done even better.

Recognise your own limitations

There are always times of the year, and certain types of tasks, where you have to accept that you are doing the best you can, and there is no point getting unduly worried and upset by limitations and shortcomings on your part. All teachers have strengths and weaknesses, and all teachers will find that some tasks require skills that are simply beyond what they have. This is illustrated by the following comment:

> I rarely get uptight although at certain times during the school year the workload becomes almost impossible – so it usually waits! I also find that pupils are much more difficult to motivate.

You also need to accept in your dealings with pupils and colleagues that there are numerous other factors at work that will influence the degree of success you can achieve. Recognising your limitations does not mean that failure is your fault. If one of your pupils just misses the required A-level grade in your subject to go to their first-choice university, or a pupil makes little progress learning to read, you need to be realistic about what you are able to achieve and to accept that there are many other people and other factors at work.

Types of coping strategies

In looking at the most frequent coping actions reported by teachers, it must be emphasised that every teacher has their own unique set of sources of stress and that every teacher needs to develop their own way of dealing with their experience of stress. For one teacher, working harder at weekends may be helpful, whilst for another it is important to spend more of their time at home relaxing; for one teacher, expressing their feelings to others is helpful, whilst for another exercising more emotional control is better. What works best for each teacher needs to take account of both their working situation and their personality. What is important is that they try to take conscious control of how they cope with the sources of stress facing them.

Indeed, Gold and Roth (1993) have argued that one cannot properly consider how a teacher can best deal with their sources of stress at work without taking careful consideration of the full range of their personal needs. They have identified three main categories of such needs: emotional–physical needs, psycho-social needs, and personal–intellectual needs; and then considered the strategies and approaches teachers can adopt to satisfy such needs in their life as a whole. In effect, they argue that the best way to help teachers deal with stress at work is to consider the 'whole person' and to help that individual to develop the skills and strategies to meet all their personal needs. One great strength of this approach is that it forces one to recognise that dealing with sources of stress at work cannot be seen in isolation from the person's whole life and the way they 'tick' as a person. Developing a teacher's ability to satisfy their personal needs will make them healthier individuals who, in turn, are better able to cope with stress at work.

An analysis of the common coping actions reported by teachers indicates that they fall into two main types. The first type are called **direct-action strategies**. Some writers have also referred to these as 'problem-solving strategies'. These involve you in identifying the source of stress and then taking action which will deal with the source of stress so that it no longer exists. In the rest of this chapter we will be looking at the various types of direct-action strategies.

The second main type of coping strategies are called **palliative strategies**. Some writers have also referred to these as 'emotion-control strategies'. Palliative strategies do not deal with the source of stress directly. Instead they try to reduce the emotional experience of stress. The source of stress is thus still there, but you come to experience less stress in its presence. Palliative strategies will be considered in the next chapter.

Preventing over-arousal

One further point to mention about coping actions, however, is that the goal of coping is not to reduce stress altogether. All important, worthwhile and challenging activities will generate some stress, and it would be difficult to imagine how it would be possible to perform such tasks well if no stress were involved. In addition, there are some tasks where a moderate degree of stress will actually enhance the quality of the performance, as it will contribute to the effort and enthusiasm you will be able to call upon. Some writers have conceptualised this as a bell-shaped curve of arousal against performance, as shown in Figure 4.1.

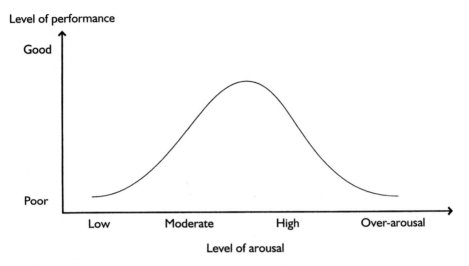

Figure 4.1 Optimal arousal

With some tasks, optimum performance will only be achieved when a moderate or high level of arousal is generated. If the task generates too little arousal, such as when you feel overconfident and bored with the task, or when you feel it is not worth making an effort to do the task well, then performance will be poor. If, however, the level of arousal is too high (over-arousal), then this can lead to a level of nervous anxiety that will impair your performance. Over-arousal can interfere with your ability to think clearly, can impair your physical coordination, and can lead you to jumping to conclusions and to over-reacting emotionally. The main aim of effective coping is thus to keep unnecessary stress to a minimum, and to prevent states of over-arousal occurring.

Direct-action strategies

In dealing with stress at work, direct-action strategies should always be used if possible. This is because direct action attempts to deal with the source of stress itself so that it is removed. The first step in using direct action is to identify as clearly as possible what is causing you stress. Having identified the source of stress, you then need to consider what action you can take so that the source of stress is removed.

For example, suppose you find there is a pupil in your class who is continually misbehaving, is disrupting the lesson for others, and you are becoming aware that this is causing you some anxiety. You now need to think of what you can do so that the pupil behaves well in future. Have you consulted colleagues to see if there is a wider problem involved? Have you checked whether the pupil is having problems with the level of the work and needs more academic support? Do you feel you need to be softer or firmer in your dealings with that pupil? Does the pupil need to be isolated within the classroom, or moved to the front? Clearly, there are many possible actions you can take. The point here is that if one of these actions works, and the pupil then starts to behave well, then the source of stress is actually removed. If you have tried different strategies and the problem persists, you could arrange for this pupil to be transferred to another class. That would effectively remove the source of stress for you, although there is a risk that it could start to generate stress for a colleague.

Another example might be that you find you are continually experiencing stress in relation to getting marking done on time. This would be an area where improving your managerial or organisational practices might be helpful. You might find that if you allocate an extra hour one evening a week, that will be adequate to deal with the marking load. Alternatively, you may decide to give less detailed feedback. Another alternative would be to arrange for more of the work to be self-assessed during the lesson. Again, if one of these actions successfully deals with the problem, then the source of stress is removed.

A third example is conflict with a colleague. If you find that you have fallen out with a colleague and that your dealings with that colleague are now generating stress, you need to consider what action you can take. For example, you could try to be overtly pleasant with that colleague, or try to clear the air in some way, or change your working practices so that you no longer need to collaborate with that colleague as often as before. Again, if one of these actions works, the source of stress is dealt with.

In general, there are five main categories of direct action:

- Direct attack.
- Enhance your skill and ability to act.
- Adapt to the situation.
- Remove the source of stress.
- Seek the help of colleagues.

Direct attack

Direct attack involves taking action in a situation where you already have the skill and ability to deal with the source of stress effectively. In this situation the task for you is simply to bring the appropriate action into play. Actions such as being firmer with a misbehaving pupil, spending more time on marking, and being friendly towards a colleague, would all be examples of direct attack. The essence of direct attack is that you identify the source of stress and then act immediately to remove it.

Direct attack is best

The greatest enemy of direct attack is an attitude of mind which encourages you to deal with problems only once they become serious and demand action. Surveys of how teachers cope with stress indicate that 'nipping problems in the bud' is one of the most frequent strategies employed.

However, the skill involved in using direct attack lies in being able to carefully match the action to the problem. Experienced teachers who have built up a repertoire of actions which they have learnt over the years are effective in dealing with certain types of situations. Consequently when a situation starts to develop which they feel needs to be 'nipped in the bud' they are immediately aware of strategies that can be brought into play. They can then select the strategy that best suits the precise features of the situation at hand (e.g. the particular type of problem, what they know about the pupils or colleagues involved, the general context, the likely consequences of different actions, how important or sensitive the problem is). In fact, one key element of teacher expertise in the area of effective stress management is this ability to precisely match an effective action to the particular situation.

The corollary of this is that direct attack does not mean than any action is better than doing nothing. A blunderbuss approach or taking the wrong action can do more harm than good, and actually make matters worse. In the early years of teaching it is therefore immensely important to be sensitive to how certain actions may lead to unintended consequences. Indeed, it may be useful to get advice from more experienced colleagues before you embark on a particular course of action.

In addition, all teachers will know that social situations involve unpredictability. A strategy which usually works effectively in a given situation may on occasions backfire. All actions need to be carefully monitored, so that if they are not having the intended effect you can quickly alter what you do. So, for example, if being firm with a pupil suddenly results in the pupil becoming tearful you need to quickly change your tone to a more caring and sympathetic manner.

Enhance your skill and ability to act

As stated, direct action can be taken immediately if you already have the skill and ability to deal successfully with the source of stress; all that is required is for you to choose the action that will be effective. However, there are many situations where you do not already have the necessary skill and ability. Indeed, that may well be the main reason for the stress occurring in the situation.

Enhancing your skill and ability to act involves taking action to change your behaviour so that in future you can deal effectively with the situation that is generating the stress. For example, if you are asked to make greater use of a particular teaching method that you are unfamiliar with, or are asked to teach a topic where you feel your subject-matter knowledge is inadequate, then this is likely to cause you some stress. However, if you can develop the new skills or areas of knowledge needed, then these sources of stress are removed. The frequent changes made to the content of the school curriculum, teaching methods and methods of assessing pupils' progress mean that teachers continually need to develop their classroom practice to keep pace with new demands.

In addition, you can easily find that the work habits that have been successful in the past are no longer effective in a new situation. For example, if the catchment for a school is changed, you may find yourself teaching pupils whose ability, attitudes and behaviour are quite different from those you typically experienced in the past. Such a change can be quite threatening for a teacher, and you may need to completely rethink your approach to lessons to take account of altered circumstances, rather than try to stick with an approach that is clearly not working for the new intake of pupils.

In a survey of teacher-stress workshops, Seidman and Zager (1992) noted that it was very important that such workshops covered areas where teachers could improve their skills in dealing with the demands and problems they face. Otherwise they could easily degenerate into 'gripe sessions'. They found that workshops which included looking at ways in which teachers could improve their teaching and classroom-management skills were particularly effective in reducing teacher stress.

Another form of action you can take involves changing your persona. All teachers gradually develop a persona of themselves as a teacher. Your persona is, in effect, the particular package of attitudes and style of behaving that you have developed to deal your work. Everyone needs to develop a persona in their occupational role. To some extent, a successful persona enables you to run on automatic pilot, as you sustain your 'teacher mode of existence' for the school day. However, from time to time you need to step back and consider whether the persona you have developed is serving you well, or making it more difficult for you to deal with sources of stress. For example, if your persona includes being very sociable and friendly towards pupils, you may find that you have allowed this to slip to the extent that pupils are able to take advantage of it by misbehaving in your lessons. You may then need to consciously make an effort to reconstruct your persona so that it better fits the needs you have for it.

The need to modify your persona is often evident when you take on new roles, particularly if these involve promotion within the school. Sometimes such a change can itself cause stress, when teachers find the new persona they need to develop feels less comfortable than the persona they used to have.

Adapt to the situation

Another approach to the situation causing you stress is to take action that enables you to adapt better to the situation that is generating the stress. Much stress that teachers experience is in part self-imposed by the standards teachers have set for their own performance. Many teachers often worry about aspects of their own performance or aspects of their pupils' work in a way that, for the most part, simply reflects the unrealistically high expectations they have set. It is clearly important that teachers and pupils are doing their best, but if the standards are set too high, then both will inevitably become frustrated and disappointed. Adapting to the situation involves taking action so that you can better match your behaviour to realistic expectations.

For example, you might find that a major source of stress for you is chasing up pupils who rarely do the homework you have set for them, and that this is generating various conflicts for you and making it difficult for you to sustain a positive rapport with the class as a whole. It may well be the case, however, that the pupils causing you this problem are very unlikely to ever do homework on a regular basis. Their attitudes towards homework may be so negative that there is more chance that conflict on this front will eventually lead to exclusion than that you will turn them into model pupils. What is more realistic is that you gradually adapt to this situation by lowering your demands on these pupils. You would continue to cajole them about the need to do homework, perhaps setting quite short tasks, and then giving praise if they are done. This may be a much more effective stance than having a series of confrontations with them. After a while, you will have reached a mutual understanding, and the problem, as a source of stress, will disappear.

Remove the source of stress

After trying various forms of direct action, you may find that the source of stress has still not been dealt with. In this situation, you may need to consider whether the source of stress can be removed or avoided in some way. The example, given earlier, of arranging for a difficult pupil to be transferred to someone else's class is relevant here.

As a teacher you will find that there are a variety of situations that, for one reason or another, are difficult to deal with despite your best endeavours to do so. For example, if you find that undertaking important organisational tasks invariably generate stress for you, you should avoid volunteering to take on any additional tasks of this sort, and see if any of the tasks you currently do could be taken on by someone else. If you find that being involved in a situation where you have to give a very strong reprimand to a pupil upsets you, you could develop alternative strategies to deal with such situations that involve referring such pupils to particular colleagues to deal with in this way. In effect, if there are sources of stress that you know cause you particular problems, and these can be avoided or dealt with better by colleagues, then you may be able to arrange for this to be done.

Seek the help of colleagues

A related approach is to seek the help of colleagues in dealing with the sources of stress facing you. This can work in two ways. First, a colleague may be able to offer you concrete help to deal with the situation. For example, they could arrange for a heavy marking load to be shared between more staff, or they could arrange for a topic area where you felt you lacked expertise to be covered in some other way.

The second way this can help is that colleagues may be able to give you practical advice on how they deal with the situation causing you stress. This might enable you to see whether part of the problem stems from your having unrealistic expectations or whether there are simply more effective actions or working practices that you are not aware of that can be brought into play. Indeed, one of the major benefits of sharing experiences with colleagues is that it can provide you with insights and possibilities for improving your practice.

Seeking advice and help

A study by Punch and Tuetteman (1996) indicated that there was also another way in which the social support teachers received from colleagues helped them reduce stress. This related to the amount of praise and recognition they received from colleagues. This finding links up with an important point made by many writers concerning work that is stressful, which is that if you feel the work you are doing is important, worthwhile and praiseworthy, that in itself somehow reduces the amount of stress you experience in doing the job. It is almost as though the sense of engaging in something which earns you praise is strong enough to neutralise any negative emotions that would otherwise have been generated. One teacher stated that before teaching a difficult class she often said to herself *'I'm off to do God's work.'* Saying this kept her cheerful and happy in the face of the difficulties she encountered. Indeed, the more difficult the class, the more she felt she was doing her duty. This point can also help explain why teachers are so sensitive to what they regard as unfair criticism about their performance or a lack of recognition from some sections of society. Just as praise and recognition can mitigate stress, unfair criticism and a lack of recognition can enhance it. This is illustrated in the following comment:

> When I have spent all evening marking, and then I hear someone saying on the news that teachers need to pull their socks up and work harder, I can feel my morale dropping like a lead balloon.

Sharing problems with colleagues can thus offer an opportunity for a teacher to receive praise for the work they are doing, thereby converting feelings of stress into feelings of satisfaction.

A study by Pithers and Soden (1998) looked at four main categories of personal activities that teachers used to alleviate stress at work:

- recreation
- self-care
- social support
- rational/cognitive thinking.

Of these, activities in the area of social support were the ones that teachers reported using most frequently. Unfortunately there is a culture that can develop in some schools, whereby teachers feel very reluctant to seek the help of colleagues in case it suggests a personal failure on their part to cope with the tasks facing them. As we will see later, a school climate in which teachers can share problems without feeling guilty can do much to minimise stress and help enhance teachers' ability to deal more effectively with the sources of stress that they do experience.

5 Palliative coping strategies

There are some sources of stress which are not readily dealt with through the use of direct action. In such cases, your best strategy is to reduce the strength of the negative emotions that are generated by such situations. Coping strategies which are aimed at reducing your subjective feeling of stress, whilst at the same time the source of stress remains present, are called palliative strategies. The following evocation nicely makes the distinction between direct-action and palliative coping strategies.

> *Give me the strength to change that which can be changed.*
> *Give me the patience to cope with that which cannot.*
> *Give me the wisdom to know the difference between the two.*

Reducing the experience of stress

In chapter 1 we looked at how stress is primarily experienced as a feeling of unpleasant negative emotions, such as tension, frustration, anger or depression. Palliative techniques are anything you can do to reduce the strength of this emotional experience. In effect, they can be regarded as emotion-control techniques. For example, in the past you may have become very upset by pupils who are disrespectful towards you. If, however, you can employ a strategy that leads to your not experiencing stress when such a situation occurs, for example disciplining yourself not to take such behaviour personally, then you are employing a palliative technique. Palliative techniques fall into two main categories: mental techniques and physical techniques.

It must be remembered however that direct-action techniques are the best ones to use, since if they are successful they actually remove the source of stress. Palliative techniques, although often very effective, will also involve a degree of mental energy to sustain effectively over a long period.

In addition, it is important to be aware that some coping actions are effective in dealing with stress, and others may be counter-productive. It is immensely important to work out what works best for you and to be sensitive to matching your coping actions to the situation you find yourself in. What works best in one situation may not be effective in another. Consequently you need to build up a repertoire of effective coping strategies and then choose the one that best fits a particular set of circumstances facing you.

A study by Salo (1995) explored teachers' use of coping actions which were categorised according to six types of strategies:

- avoidance of thinking
- problem-solving
- social support
- thinking about work alone
- devoting oneself to free-time activities
- the use of food, alcohol or tobacco.

The findings of this study indicated that avoidance of thinking about work and directing your thoughts to outside interests such as hobbies were the coping actions most associated with lower levels of stress. In contrast, certain actions, such as excessive alcohol consumption, were indicative of high levels of stress. Studies such as that reported by Salo highlight three important points.

First, a useful distinction can be made between *adaptive* coping and *maladaptive* coping. The former is effective in reducing stress whilst the latter is not. Maladaptive coping actions tend to be things you can do that offer very quick and short-term relief from stress but are counter-productive in the longer term. For example, losing your temper can sometimes feel good for a moment because it offers a pleasurable release of built-up emotion, but the consequences are likely to include the creation of a host of new problems. Similarly, bingeing on food may feel great at the time, but you are likely to feel ill afterwards, and if you start to put on weight as well, that can also make it harder for you to deal with stress (both physically and by lowering your self-image).

Too much coffee may make you frazzled

Second, just because a coping action is used frequently does not mean it must be effective. As a teacher it is very easy to acquire bad habits, and to resort to these frequently in a stereotyped, unthinking manner. For example, when experiencing stress it might be easy to resort to drinking a strong cup of coffee. Having a cup of coffee is fine, but if during periods when high demands are made on you, you start to drink several cups a day, you may well find that such a high intake of caffeine will heighten your feelings of tension and make you more likely to feel frazzled when problems arise. In such a situation, you would be well advised to switch to caffeine-free coffee. Whilst caffeine-free coffee will give you less of the immediate and more pleasurable buzz, it will better enable you to sustain a feeling of being relaxed. At the same, by drinking caffeine-free coffee you can still engage in the pleasant social exchanges that take place between colleagues at break times, which are often the real reason why coffee breaks are seen as helpful in reducing stress.

Understanding yourself

Your ability to cope effectively with stress will be enhanced by understanding what type of person you are and how this relates to your experience of stress. Because we all have a different psychological make-up and a different personal history of events that have happened to us in our lives, we all have a unique profile that reflects how we appraise our circumstances and how we respond to the perception of threat to our self-esteem or well-being. Gray and Freeman (1987) highlight seven aspects to understanding yourself that have importance for your use of coping strategies. These points, which are listed below, are particularly relevant to the use of palliative strategies.

- consistent personality
- emotional colouring
- being fed up
- identity and self-esteem
- feedback and coping
- social support.

Gray and Freeman argue that our personality tends to predispose us to respond to certain events in a fairly similar way. By being aware of how your personality can make you vulnerable to seeing certain situations as stressful and can predispose you to respond to these in a stereotyped way, you will be able to develop a broader and more effective range of coping strategies. For example, a major enemy of effective coping is responding too quickly and uncritically to the events facing you. If you know you tend to be impulsive, then a very important strategy is to curtail your impulsiveness by employing strategies which help you to delay your tendency to make decisions on the hoof. The advice to 'sleep on it' before making an important decision reflects this approach.

Your personality will also influence the emotional colouring you put on situations. Optimistic people will tend to look at things in a positive light; phlegmatic people will tend to be more sanguine about events; affectionate people will tend to find that their feeling are easily hurt if they feel a pupil or a colleague has let them down personally. All events are emotionally coloured by the sort of person we are, and that colouring will affect our interpretation of those events.

Gray and Freeman highlight the mood of 'being fed up' in the battle against stress. We can also fall into periods when we feel mildly depressed, and start to see those around us as blameworthy for this. When we feel fed up, we are also prone to find that what would otherwise be quite trivial matters further reinforce our sense of depression. All teachers need to be alert to this type of mood, and develop palliative strategies to lift themselves from it as soon as it seems to have developed. Your personality also affects how you appraise whether an event threatens your identity or self-esteem. One teacher said to me:

> I have been a teacher for 15 years, and generally speaking I have enjoyed being a teacher. I like teaching and I like the kids. However, all this meaningless and ill thought out paperwork I keep being asked to do really annoys me. I didn't come into teaching to spend hours doing paperwork.

The last sentence reflects the fact that most people have an image of themselves doing a job which in part needs to match their sense of personal identity and self-esteem. If they find that their work no longer provides a good match, they will start to feel very uncomfortable about this. Another example of this would be a teacher who has authoritarian tendencies, and likes their classes to be very ordered and well regulated. If such a teacher starts to find that the pupils they are teaching are too unruly compared with their image of how they would like things to be, this again would make that teacher vulnerable to seeing this as a source of stress.

Gray and Freeman also highlight the importance of using feedback to improve coping strategies. Feedback from other teachers, from pupils or from other sources, enables you to appreciate your strengths and weaknesses as a teacher, and to enhance and develop those skills that will help you deal more effectively with the demands being made. Using such feedback effectively may also provide you with a more precise understanding of the factors that lead to the situation generating stress for you. For example, if you are upset by a pupil who reacted violently against you, you might find this was because you took the event personally. If you discover the pupil has been causing even worse problems in other classes, or that the cause is very much based on emotional traumas occurring in that pupil's home life, you will probably find that the occurrence of a similar event a few weeks later with the same pupil will be much less stressful to deal with.

Predictability can also influence our response to situations. For example, knowing that you have to teach a very difficult pupil may lead to stress building up in anticipation of the event. Similarly, an unpredictable event can generate a high level of stress, in part because the shock value of not being prepared for the event may have caught your coping strategies by surprise.

Finally, Gray and Freeman emphasise that the presence of social support, through talking with colleagues and sharing experiences, can have a major impact on reducing stress. In contrast, the absence of social support, particularly if you feel isolated, can enhance feelings of stress.

Mental techniques

Mental techniques are anything you can do to alter how you view the situation. Stress is triggered by your perception of a threat to your self-esteem or well-being. If you can come to view the situation in a way that sees it as less threatening, then that will mitigate the experience of stress. The four key mental techniques used by teachers are:

- Put things in perspective.
- See the humour in the situation.
- Think of positive things.
- Emotion control.

Put things in perspective

The most powerful mental technique is to put things in perspective. It is very easy in the hustle and bustle of everyday life in school to get things out of perspective and to become upset by an incident that is really quite trivial. For example, if a pupil draws a diagram in ink instead of in pencil, despite your explicit advice to the whole class not to do so, you might find yourself becoming quite angry. However, this is not the end of Western civilisation as we know it. Many such incidents are just part and parcel of school life, and you need to remind yourself that many incidents that cause stress are really quite trivial in the scheme of things.

Putting things in perspective is well illustrated by the following comment.

> I did not become a teacher until 40 years of age. Prior to that I worked in a hospital, and I found that very stressful. Sometimes when I face a problem at school, I just think of the things I saw happening in hospital and I find my problems at school seem to be a relief to deal with by comparison. I just feel so thankful now that I don't have to worry about life and death issues all the time.

This comment also conveys how other life experiences can help teachers to put events at school in a truer perspective. Experience in teaching can also help you realise that the consequences of certain events will not be half as serious as you might think.

See the humour in the situation

Another powerful mental technique is to see the humour in the situation. A pupil who refuses to do any work can remind you of yourself when you were young and were sometimes frustrated and felt you wanted to rebel against authority. Thinking along these lines can quickly transform your feelings from threat and anger to empathy towards that pupil. You may also see the situation as quite humorous. Indeed, with so many demands on teachers nowadays, a sense of humour is probably a prerequisite for staying sane. One of the benefits of a healthy level of humorous banter in the staffroom at break times is that it helps teachers to dissipate some of the stress that has been building up during the day. This point is made in the following comment:

> This, I believe, is an excellently organised school, mainly due to the amount of paperwork that is processed. Nevertheless, this involves meeting deadlines and this often creates a real stress situation. A radical approach would be to develop a system similar to that in France. Let administrators administer, teachers teach, and supervisors supervise. Much of this might be relieved if teachers were not expected to double as managers, detectives, social workers, probation officers, parents, marriage guidance counsellors, etc. I have a dry sense of humour which, fortunately, is shared by my immediate colleagues. I really look forward to the daily dose of good humour that permeates the staffroom at break times (most days at any rate!) and I am sure that I would not still be in teaching if I were not at a school where I had so many good friends.

Think of positive things

Another useful technique is to have positive thoughts you can turn to. For example, if you have interests outside school which you enjoy, you can periodically think about these during the school day, and sometimes talk about them with colleagues. This is illustrated in the following comment:

> Large schools and large classes do not allow you to develop individual relationships with pupils which are vital for cooperative learning. In this school, I find teaching involves a lot of effort for very little return. In contrast, the work I do for the Girl Guides Association gives me a lot of satis-

faction. When I get stressed at school, I sometimes think of things I am planning to do with the Girl Guides and that helps keep me sane.

Thinking about positive things in this way from time to time can help you feel much more positive about the things going on around you.

This technique is linked to the idea of emotion control, outlined below.

Emotion control

Emotion control tries to ensure that you do not allow your feelings to get out of control. There are two main ways of doing this. The first is to tell yourself to keep calm. This can be enhanced by using physical techniques to help keep your body relaxed. If you know what type of situations are likely to generate stress for you, then you can to some extent forewarn yourself of the need to stay calm.

The second key way of maintaining emotion control is to curtail spending long periods ruminating about your problems. Some people spend far too long mentally replaying over and over again an unpleasant event that has occurred and thinking about the unfairness, injustice and hurtfulness of the experience. Sometimes this type of rumination long after the event can work you up into a state that is far worse than your original response when the event first occurred. The ability not to ruminate for long periods is a useful mental technique for stress reduction. To prevent yourself engaging in such rumination, you can simply tell yourself that the event is over and past and that there is little value in thinking about it further and, then, at that point engage your mind in some other activity, such as reading a book, watching television, baking a cake or going out for a meal. Many types of physical activity, such as playing squash or being in a choir, are particularly effective in helping you to direct your mind away from needless rumination. This is illustrated by the following comment:

I belong to a choir. Singing is a great activity for relieving stress, because it occupies you both physically and mentally, so it really takes you out of yourself. I wouldn't give it up now for the world. I used to feel a bit guilty at first, as I thought I ought to be doing other things, but in the long run I am sure it has made me a happier person both at home and at school.

A study by Roger and Hudson (1995) indicates that training people to achieve emotion control by combining these two strategies of relaxation and curtailing rumination can be very effective in reducing stress at work. Interestingly, they also argue that having a low self-esteem may be linked to a tendency to rumination and, consequently, any activities or experiences which can enhance a person's feelings of self-esteem may lead to a reduction in rumination and thereby a reduction in their experience of stress. This may in part explain why

Hobbies help take your mind off work

receiving praise from colleagues can be effective in reducing a teacher's experience of stress.

There are, however, some other mental techniques involved in emotion control that can have mixed results or may even be unhealthy in the long run. One such technique is that of maintaining an emotional detachment from events at work. This strategy involves you in trying to maintain an emotional distance from incidents. You try to behave in as professional a manner as possible, but you retain a sense of cold detachment from events which are causing you concern. For example, if a pupil fails to do their homework, you tell yourself that you have taken the appropriate action and there is no point in getting personally worried and upset about this situation. There are some occupations, such as social work, nursing and the police service, where the ability to detach yourself emotionally from certain events that you are dealing with is sometimes quite important. However, in teaching, such a detachment can impact badly on your ability to deal with problems that occur, and this needs to be exercised with particular care.

Related to the idea of detachment is the mental technique of compartmentalisation. This involves you in mentally separating out different areas of your work, and trying not to think of issues related to one area when you are engaged in work in another area. One of the major sources of panic teachers sometimes report experiencing can be the feeling that they are simply so overloaded that their thoughts about other tasks keep intruding on their current activity. The ability to mentally set aside your thinking about other tasks can prevent this sense of overload panic occurring.

A more extreme mental technique is denial. This involves simply denying to yourself at a subconscious level that you are having problems that are causing you stress. This is an unhealthy technique to employ, as it impairs your ability to use direct-action techniques, it requires a great deal of mental effort to sustain, and invariably allows the problem to get worse.

Physical techniques

Physical techniques are things you can do that physically reduce the feelings of tension and frustration that are generated when you experience stress. The report of the Education Service Advisory Committee (1998) identified three main physical techniques:

- relaxation techniques
- exercise
- medication.

During the school day, there are techniques you can employ that will enable you to realise that your body is tense and to help it relax. These can include breathing exercises. Indeed, many teachers are unaware just how tense their muscles can become during the school day. Any exercises that enable you to recognise this and to relax will be very helpful.

After school, the main physical techniques involve relaxing your body by winding down physical activity, or getting rid of stress-related tension by engaging in rigorous exercise.

Medication to relieve anxiety may be helpful for some teachers in the short term, but more effective coping techniques must be brought into play so that the use of medication can be terminated at the earliest possible opportunity.

Physical techniques are very important in coping with stress because many of the signs of stress that will convey to others (such as colleagues and pupils) that you are experiencing a high level of stress stem from the physical consequences of being very tense and anxious. This can include a shrill voice, not being able to find things, having clenched teeth and hands, and sweating. Knowing that others can see you are experiencing stress can in turn generate more stress for you. Consequently if you can develop techniques to get your body to feel relaxed when facing sources of stress, this will help prevent the development of

a vicious circle of stress leading to more stress, and instead start to generate a virtuous circle of recovery.

The five key physical techniques used by teachers are:

- Reduce bodily tension in school.
- Take breaks in school.
- Relax after school.
- Exercise after school.
- Pamper yourself after school.

Reduce bodily tension in school

Relaxation training programmes are designed to help you become aware of
when your muscles are tense and to get used to the feeling of how to relax them.
The training sessions usually involve you in sitting or lying comfortably and
then thinking of something very relaxing. You then tense up a particular mus-
cle and after a while you let it relax. You gradually do this for a whole series of
muscles in your body (neck, back, legs, etc.). Thereafter, when you are in a situation in which you experience stress, you can take conscious control to enable
your muscles to relax.

An extension of this technique is one whereby you mentally try to sustain the
physical feeling of relaxation at the same time as you imagine yourself in the situation that is causing you stress. By doing this at home, when you are able to
relax easily, you can gradually become desensitised to the particular source of
stress you have been using in your imagery.

Some teacher training courses have used such imagery techniques in their
training sessions. In some cases, this has then been extended to role-play situations, in which the student teachers attempt to stay relaxed in a situation that
would normally generate stress. Examples of such role-play situations are con-
fronting a group of pupils you are sure have cheated during an examination,
and explaining to an upset parent why you have not marked their child's work
for some time. The idea here is that if teachers can learn how to stay relaxed in
such situations, they are generally much better able to deal with a difficult situation effectively without experiencing a high level of stress.

Take breaks in school

Taking a break by sitting down and having a cup of tea or coffee all helps the
body to recover, although, as noted in the last chapter, you do need to monitor
your intake of caffeine, as a high intake will almost certainly lead to your feeling more tense. The main benefit of taking such breaks is that they allow your
body to relax and also provide you with some critical distance from your imme-

diate problems. The healthy banter and social interaction that commonly occurs in staffrooms during break time also helps to enhance this feeling of relief and reduction in tension. It also produces an opportunity to share a problem with a colleague, or to show and receive support through empathy. This is illustrated by the following comment:

> I find teaching a job which demands a lot. The job is hard because many pupils won't allow me to teach. I love teaching but feel that I actually teach rarely. I mostly child mind and control potential riots. Most of my colleagues are quite young, so as a fairly new teacher myself I feel I get a lot of help and understanding from them, including some useful tips during the lunch break and reassurance that things will get a lot easier as I get more experience.

Anyone who is too busy to take a break should regard this as a warning sign that they are doing too much. We all experience days when there is just too much to deal with, and one task or train of thought keeps getting interrupted by each new set of demands. No one can sustain this pace of work, day after day, without running a real risk of ill health. In many occupations breaks are compulsory, in the sense that everyone takes them when they are due. In some occupations, such as teaching, it is very easy to allow tasks to be dealt with at break times. Indeed, there are many tasks, such as checking something with a colleague, that are best done at break times. However, what you must guard against is occupying yourself with so many tasks at break times that you find yourself going without breaks.

Relax after school

The following comment well illustrates how some teachers feel that they are spending too much time doing school-related work during the evening.

> The work is often exhausting and overruns into family and social life. Marking frequently has to be done at home, as well as preparation. Parents evenings etc. seem to be grouped very close together and consequently some weeks nearly all of your waking hours are spent in or around school.

It is extremely important for all teachers to find some time during the evening to relax. At the end of the school day, when you get home, there are things you can do to unwind such as having a relaxing bath, listening to some relaxing music, immersing yourself in a hobby, and having a nice meal. All of these will help you to quickly get your body back to a state of relaxation.

A number of writers have also pointed to the benefits of engaging in meditation exercises. Fontana (1989) points to four key benefits:

- It trains the attention.
- It increases control over thought processes.
- It increases the ability to handle emotions.
- It aids physical relaxation.

The essence of meditation lies in developing the ability of the mind to remain focused in a relaxed way on a particular object, sound or idea you have chosen. In doing this, you gradually become aware of how other thoughts creep in and how these need to be denied attention. After a while you become used to this sensation of being able to direct and sustain your attention on a particular object. This provides you with an awareness of how your mind can easily jump from one train of thinking to another when you are bombarded with different demands. Meditation allows you to control your thinking better, so that you can avoid the sense of panic that can arise in a stressful situation when you feel your thoughts are getting out of control. Meditation also has a calming effect on the body and can help dissipate any feelings of tension and frustration that have built up during the school day. To benefit from meditation, it is important to practise it regularly, even if it is only for a few minutes each morning or evening.

Fontana (1989) points out that another useful technique involving meditation is to get into a state of relaxation and then to think about a situation that upsets you, whilst maintaining the feeling of relaxation at the same time. In doing this, you can develop a feeling of detaching the negative emotion from the situation that upsets you. You then come to appreciate how a feeling of negative emotion is something that you have induced in yourself – it is not an inherent property of the situation. This realisation enables you to gradually develop more control over what emotion you will allow a situation to generate. For most people, the emotional response to a situation occurs so quickly, they naturally come to think that the emotion is almost part of the situation. The realisation that we can mentally intervene between a situation and our emotional response to it can have a profound effect on improving the effectiveness of coping actions.

Exercise after school

Some teachers who get home tired naturally assume that they need to relax. However, an important distinction needs to be made between being mentally tired and being physically tired. If you have been teaching most of the day and have been rushing around, the likelihood is that you feel both mentally and physically tired. However, there are some times when although you have had a mentally demanding day, your body has not been particularly active physically. This is particularly likely if you have been doing a lot of administrative work, preparation or marking during the day, but have not been very active in your classroom teaching. In this way, you may arrive home with thoughts and ideas spinning around in your head, but when you sit down to relax you find your body still feels very tensed up. In such circumstances physical activity, such as going for a brisk walk, can help the body unwind and help you to relax as the evening develops.

In addition, taking part in physical sports, such as swimming or playing squash, and other leisure activities, such as singing or gardening, can all help you keep your body in good shape whilst at the same time dissipating any feelings of tension that may have been generated by demands at work.

Pamper yourself after school

Another important way in which you can relieve the feelings of stress is to indulge yourself in things you enjoy doing. It is very important to realise that you are the only person who genuinely knows what you really enjoy doing. No one else can be sure that the activities they arrange for you to give you pleasure are the things you really enjoy. In addition, it is easy to fall into the trap of being so busy looking after the needs of other people and making sure they are happy, that you neglect your own needs.

Pampering yourself occasionally is an important way of relieving stress

From time to time it is important for you to think about things that give you pleasure and then to set these activities up for yourself. It might include going out for a nice meal, going to the theatre, a shopping weekend in another city, seeing some friends, or a walk in the countryside. You need to make time for yourself to do those things you know you enjoy doing.

Sometimes these activities can be expensive. However, pampering yourself in this way will enhance the pleasure you get. Why not stay in a top-class hotel for a weekend? Why not buy an elegant new item of clothing? In many cases you can well afford to do such things from time to time, and the only thing stopping you is that you have not taken time out to plan to do them. Unless you get your diary out and fix a time for these things to happen, weeks, months or even years can pass without your doing them. Part of better managing stress at work involves you in better managing your life as a whole and making sure you pamper yourself from time to time. Such activities will help you sustain a sense of well-being in your life that will make you less likely to experience stress when faced with a problem that needs to be dealt with.

A healthy personal life

Many teachers report that it is difficult not to bring home problems that arise at work. This concern is illustrated in the following comment:

> Frustration at the lack of support and indeed inability of those people higher up on the administrative side to provide same. A feeling of fighting the battle for high standards, both academic and disciplinary – alone. This eliminates satisfaction derived from teaching able and interested children. This impacts on my private life. Inability to shut the door at 4 p.m.

Whilst there are times when it makes sense not to 'shut the door at 4 p.m.' there are also times when this is important if you are to achieve a healthy balance between your work and your home life. In addition, however, you need to think about how well you deal with problems arising in your home life. There can be times when the demands on you at home are more pressing and important than those facing you at work, and you need to give these the attention they deserve.

Stress generated at home can easily spill over into the workplace, and vice versa. A study by Sheffield *et al.* (1994) indicated that there was a strong association between the level of stress teachers reported at work and their reported level of life stress in general. Such data cannot, of course, clearly indicate the main direction of causality. What the data do highlight, however, is the need for you to ensure that you do not allow problems at work to distract you from the importance of sustaining your personal relationships with others at home. It is also important not to take a healthy home life for granted, and allow the quality of your home life to be gradually undermined by the demands made on you at work. Home life will inevitably have its ups and downs, so when things are going well at home, remember to keep something in reserve so that you have the time and energy to deal with periods when life at home is going less well.

A number of writers have also looked at the particular problems related to dual-career relationships, where both partners have a full-time job. As with all relationships that work well, the lifestyles and attitudes of the partners need to be compatible and complementary. If both you and your partner are working, your expectations of each other's role in the relationship have to take account of this. There will be times when you need to provide emotional support and empathy for your partner when they experience stress at work, just as you can reasonably expect your partner to reciprocate when you are facing problems at work. Cartwright and Cooper (1997) have highlighted the importance in dual-career relationships of ensuring that family tensions are reduced, and of dealing with marital problems that are generated when one or more of the partners are showing signs of stress. Such writers indicate that the main points of guidance are:

- Find time to talk to each other in a relaxed way.
- Communicate with your partner in a way that is not accusatory.
- Listen carefully to what your partner says and respond in a way that shows you have listened and empathise.
- Help your partner to focus on positive action they can take to deal with stress at work.
- Don't let your partner's experience of stress at work infect your feelings.
- Don't take out your feeling of stress at work on your partner.
- Don't get drawn into endless rows.
- Make time to enjoy activities together.
- Be ready to take on extra household tasks to help your partner out when they are under pressure, and ask your partner to do the same for you.
- Let your partner know if you are having problems rather than assume they can tell.

This last point is particularly important. Some people assume that their partner ought to, in some magical way, know when they are having problems at work, and expect them to be particularly supportive and helpful during such times. When their partner is not supportive in the expected way, they become resentful and may accuse them of not caring, when in fact the partner simply did not recognise that they had had a particularly stressful day. Consequently it is a good idea to let your partner know how you feel if you come home upset or worried by events at work, so that they can be alerted to your need for support.

A number of writers have also pointed out the importance of having a healthy diet. People who do jobs which involve a lot of rushing around, and who get home tired at the end of the day, are prone to develop bad eating habits. They are likely to rush their meals, or miss them altogether, and to eat snacks and convenience foods rather than freshly cooked meals.

Gold and Roth (1993) suggest that teachers need to develop a 'personal life plan' to manage stress at work effectively. Part of doing this, they suggest, is to monitor your physical state of health by keeping a journal of what you do each day in the areas of:

- eating
- exercise
- relaxation.

At the end of each week you can then draw up a list of 'what I learnt statements', and then draw up a list of things you will do to improve matters. For example, the 'I learnt statements' might include:

- I eat too much junk food.
- I eat on the run.
- I seldom take time to relax.

Eat freshly cooked food

The action statements might include:

- I will take a walk after dinner at least five times a week.
- I will go to a weight-control club.

Fontana (1989) recommends that teachers should try to maintain a healthy diet as part of managing stress. In particular, teachers should:

- eat plenty of fresh fruit and vegetables
- eat plenty of fibre
- eat freshly cooked food
- avoid eating too much sugar and salt
- avoid eating too much fat, especially saturated fats.

Mills (1990), in her stress-management guide for teachers, uses the notion of 'stressproofing through lifestyle' to highlight how a healthy lifestyle can help reduce your vulnerability to stress. These stressproofing activities focus on:

- your physical condition: exercise, diet, rest, relaxation
- your mental condition: activities that take your mind off work and help you to switch off
- your emotional condition: activities that reaffirm your priorities in life and help you face and solve problems.

In her guide, Mills has highlighted 27 stressproofing activities or qualities, shown in the box below.

A healthy lifestyle

Good diet   Regular exercise   Cut down the coffee

Fresh air   Correct weight   Health checks

Massage   Low alcohol level   Pacing yourself

Preparation for sound sleep   No smoking   Relaxation

Setting boundaries   Socialising   Change

Hobbies   Monitoring stress   Self-forgiveness

Building bridges   Asking for help   Targeting

Optimism   Sense of humour   Laughing

Calm   Assertiveness   Personal space and time

Mills goes on to offer advice on preparing yourself to sleep for those who have problems going to sleep or who have interrupted sleep patterns. These include:

- Never try to sleep after a mental activity – switch off first.
- Try a short stroll before bedtime.
- Avoid coffee, alcohol and smoking before bedtime, which are all stimulants – warm milk is better.
- Only go to bed when you are tired, which will help you to associate bed with sleep.
- Avoid sleeping tablets.
- Get up at the same time each day so that you develop and maintain a regular body clock.

If when you go to bed you find that you are still too mentally alert to nod off, you should try some mental-relaxation strategies to help your mind wander off, such as imagining yourself going for a stroll, or thinking about the sensation of your muscles being relaxed. If you still fail to fall asleep, you should get up and do something to help you relax, and then try again later.

It is interesting to note the word 'calm' in Mills's list of stressproofing activities, as many books on coping with stress at work have highlighted techniques that people can use to stay calm. One of the most popular writers adopting this approach is Wilson (1998). He argues that the most important decision facing you if you are to be successful in reducing stress at work is to make the commitment that you will implement various stress-reduction strategies. Reading and thinking about such strategies may provide useful ideas, but you must make a firm commitment that you will actually use these techniques.

For Wilson, the most powerful technique is to practise meditation. Another important technique he highlights is based on the idea of selflessness. Wilson advocates that each day you should try and do something to help another person, particularly someone less fortunate than yourself. Wilson argues that doing this helps you to overcome the self-centred nature of your own stress. Another important technique advocated by Wilson is to use various mental devices to maintain a positive, happy and optimistic outlook on life.

Developing your personal coping actions

You can now look again at the ten main sources of stress facing you that you were asked to list at the end of chapter 2. For each of these sources of stress, you should now consider which coping actions might be effective in dealing with them. Remember to think about using direct-action techniques first, and to consider palliative techniques as back-up or for additional support.

Table 5.1 illustrates how one teacher might do this. All the examples in the table are taken from the responses of teachers taking part in workshops I have run on teacher stress. Do this now.

Table 5.1 A personal action plan for coping

Do this!

Source of stress	Action
1. I worry about the need to use more ICT in my teaching before the next Ofsted inspection.	Arrange for some sessions with the ICT coordinator to take place during the half-term break.
2. I spend too many evenings marking pupils' work.	Will stay on at school for half-an-hour on Tuesday and Thursdays and get some marking done in the staffroom.
3. Not enough textbooks.	Get things in perspective – there are plenty of worksheets and extra textbooks are due for delivery soon.
4. Covering lessons for absent colleagues.	Ask Head to explore using more supply cover or to look at other alternatives.
5. Some pupils seem to lack interest in the work.	I need to have more realistic expectations about what I can achieve.
6. I get upset when I think about what was said about my teaching in my appraisal statement.	I must stop ruminating about this – the statement was overall very good, and the one comment that could be interpreted negatively was probably not meant in a negative sense anyway.
7. The Head keeps asking me to help set up an outward bound activity – I hate that type of activity.	I must stop prevaricating and tell the Head that this type of activity is just not my scene.
8. I feel hurt when I think about the fact that my idea of setting up a debating group just gets no support from colleagues.	I can do this alone for a term and see how things go.
9. The government keeps introducing changes to the school curriculum at short notice.	This is just something I need to accept is the way things are nowadays and do the best I can in the time and with the resources available.
10. Helping a younger colleague out who keeps having discipline problems.	Arrange for two particularly difficult pupils to be transferred out of the younger colleague's class and see if the deputy head can be involved in providing additional support and advice.

6 What schools can do to minimise stress

As well as action that teachers can take to reduce their own individual stress, there is much that school managers can do to ensure that the level of stress experienced by staff is kept as low as possible.

The Education Service Advisory Committee (1998) identified a number of aspects of the management role in reducing teacher stress:

- group problem solving
- developing a supportive culture
- information and training
- occupational health services
- employee assistance schemes.

The report of the Health Education Authority (1988) made the following recommendations for reducing teacher stress:

- Construct clear job descriptions which avoid ambiguity.
- Develop effective selection procedures.
- Develop staff induction programmes for new teachers and for experienced teachers promoted to senior posts.
- Provide continuing staff development.
- Improve the physical work environment; for example reduce noise levels.
- Encourage each school to establish its own whole-school and tailor-made stress-reduction programmes, if necessary calling on expert advice.
- Examine and clarify the roles of local education authorities to reduce the delays and frustrations caused by role confusion and unnecessary bureaucracy and improve coordination between schools and authorities.

The healthy school

A useful way of thinking about how schools can help to reduce teacher stress is to think of how well they resemble the characteristics of a healthy school. These can be identified as follows:

- There are good communications between staff.
- There is a strong sense of collegiality.

- Management decisions are based on consultation.
- Consensus is established on key values and standards.
- Whole-school policies are in place.
- Roles and expectations are clearly defined.
- Teachers receive positive feedback and praise.
- Teachers are supported by a good level of resources and facilities.
- Support is available to help solve problems.
- Policies and procedures are easy to follow.
- Red tape and paperwork are minimised.
- Additional duties are matched to teachers' skills.
- The building environment is pleasant to work in.
- Senior management makes good use of forward planning.
- Induction and career development advice is given.

Similarly, in her treatment of 'Stressproofing Your School', Mills (1990) describes the ideal school as exhibiting the following ten characteristics:

- clear aims and objectives
- excellent communication system
- a sensible approach to time, deadlines and workload
- a pleasant working environment
- little ill-health and low absenteeism
- high levels of morale and motivation
- a good image in the community
- consistent and effective teamwork
- feelings of membership and loyalty in staff and pupils
- few conflicts between people.

All the teacher unions have published reports on teacher stress analysing the problems facing teachers and offering advice and guidance on how schools can help reduce stress. A number of these have focused on the characteristics of organisational health as a means of helping schools to provide a better working environment for teachers. A good example of this is the NUT (1990) document which outlines an action plan for organisational health that can provide an effective programme to tackle teacher stress. This action plan deals with three key areas: the task environment, the problem-solving and the social environment, and the development environment. The NUT action plan is as follows:

I The task environment

This section deals with the situation facing teachers as they attempt to do their work. It identifies the need to:

- design jobs and allocate duties such that teachers' skills are better matched to the demands on them

- reduce time pressures and introduce time-management training
- provide more non-contact time for preparation and marking
- make greater use of teaching and administrative assistants
- improve the physical environment and provide more teaching resources
- reduce class size
- provide better training on the management of disruptive pupils and more support in dealing with them
- work towards increased agreement on 'aims and objectives' of the school.

Effective teamwork is important

2 Problem solving and the social environment

This section deals with how well the school works together as a team to deal with problems. It identifies the need to:

- develop a more cooperative and supportive culture
- provide time and opportunities for staff to relax together

- improve the cohesiveness and quality of the social environment
- develop the idea of team problem solving
- legitimise this idea by providing time for staff to discuss problems together
- improve communication within the school
- provide better feedback to teachers
- request senior teachers to share information more readily.

3 The development environment

This section deals with how well the school develops its staff both as individuals and as teachers. It identifies the need to:

- develop better person management within schools
- improve leadership and management styles adopted by headteachers and deputies
- make more frequent and better use of expressions of appreciation of teachers' efforts and achievements
- work towards more frequent and better use of feedback
- improve initial and in-service training, making it relevant to their real needs; include management training for headteachers, stress and time management, training in communication skills and in the management of disruptive pupils
- seek to provide better support facilities for staff within schools, including a broadly based organisational health service, counselling and leisure facilities
- make efforts to improve community and public perception of teachers.

The report of the Education Service Advisory Committee (1998) argued that senior managers in a school who adopt a positive policy towards health at work can have a major impact on reducing levels of teacher stress. The report highlighted how managers may need to draw up action plans to tackle the stress generated by different aspects of the school culture, such as:

- training, induction and professional development
- the classroom situation (workload, resources, relations with disruptive pupils)
- the physical work environment
- school organisation (management style, communications)
- external factors (political and community expectations)
- administration (spreading the load, providing simple systems).

Similarly, the report of the Health Education Authority (1988) highlighted how inadequacies in three areas of management skills by headteachers or deputy heads were commonly cited by teachers as creating stress. These three areas were:

Leadership skills. On the one hand some headteachers and deputy heads failed to give a lead to staff, and were unclear or inconsistent about the school's overall aims, policies and practices and their expectations of staff. On the other hand, some headteachers or deputy heads behaved in an autocratic manner, over-relying on rules, failing to consult and leaving little scope for staff to show initiative.

Practical skills. The problems here stem largely from inadequacies in organising and coordinating the work of other teachers, failing to communicate important information in good time, or carrying out important tasks badly or leaving them undone altogether.

Interpersonal skills. Senior managers need to be able to exert their authority by maintaining a good balance between ordering/insisting on the one hand and persuading/advising on the other hand. Senior managers without the appropriate social skills to do this may cause problems for other staff.

The Health Education Authority has argued strongly for all senior managers in schools to receive appropriate management training both before and after gaining such senior posts within schools.

The induction of new staff

Dunham (1992), in his analysis of how schools can improve their organisational resources to reduce teacher stress, has paid particular attention to the importance of having in place a good induction programme for new members of staff. Both newly qualified teachers and more experienced teachers moving to a new school need help to adjust smoothly to working in a new organisation. Whilst many writers have pointed to the need for an induction programme to help newly qualified teachers, much less attention has been given to the similar needs of more experienced staff, including the appointment of headteachers.

It is well recognised that newly qualified teachers face many demands in their first year as full-time teachers. A study by Cains and Brown (1998) of stress amongst newly qualified teachers asked them to rate the factors that had been most useful in helping them to cope with stress. They reported that the extent of perceived support which is provided by informal advice from colleagues was far and away seen to be the most useful factor. Similarly, studies of how newly appointed headteachers and deputy heads adjust to a new school and their new role also point to the importance of the support and advice they receive informally from other headteachers and deputy heads (Dunham, 1992).

Unfortunately, the quality of the support given to new staff will vary from school to school, and can in large measure depend on the extent to which members of the existing staff volunteer to offer such support. Consequently, having in place a more formal induction programme for new staff, including the appointment of a mentor with whom you are encouraged to consult and who will take a proactive role in ensuring your needs are met, will provide an organisational framework in which a good level of support will be available. In the case of senior appointments, such as headteachers or deputy heads, the main support and the appointment of a mentor may well come from senior staff in other schools as part of an induction programme for senior staff organised through professional associations and/or by the local education authority.

The induction needs facing new staff fall into two categories. First, there is simply getting to grips with a knowledge and understanding of the school and how it operates. This includes everything from what the pupils are like to where you go to collect paper clips. Meeting these information needs may take the form of briefings and being given a copy of relevant documentation. The information needs of new staff are listed in the box below.

The information needs of new staff

Your job description

Your immediate 'line manager'

Brief history of the school and its catchment

Copy of the school prospectus

School buildings and layout

Access to resources

School organisation

Role responsibilities of different members of staff

School decision-making processes and procedures

Whole-school policies and procedures

Pastoral care system

Liaison arrangements with other staff

Dealing with medical emergencies

Appointment of a mentor

Arrangements for reports and assessment

Sources of advice and support

Teacher appraisal scheme

Professional development activities

Second, there are those needs involved in dealing with all the demands facing you in your new role that relate to the quality of your teaching, administration, and managerial tasks. These are best seen in terms of the questions people need to ask themselves about how they are doing their job.

In relation to meeting the performance concerns of newly qualified teachers, the Teacher Training Agency (1999) has proposed that all schools establish an 'induction tutor' whose primary role will be to assist in the professional development of newly qualified teachers during their induction period, and in particular to build on those performance needs identified in their 'career entry profile'.

With regard to the induction needs for more experienced teachers, a number of schools have a member of staff who is given special responsibility for staff development. This clearly overlaps with teacher appraisal and with the headteacher's monitoring of staff performance more generally. It is certainly important for schools to ensure that the needs of a new teacher do not fall between different stools, or, conversely, that a new teacher is not bombarded with different types of monitoring arrangements.

With regard to new headteachers, schemes such as 'Headlamp' (the Headteachers' Leadership and Management Programme) provide a structured induction programme for new, first-time headteachers, and also point to the type of support and advice such new headteachers will need from others and, in particular, from the school's governing body. Ostell and Oakland (1995), in their study of headteacher stress, noted that there were many problem situations that headteachers could only deal with successfully with the help of others. First-time headteachers are likely to need particular help as they will be dealing with many types of situation for the first time, and will not be aware of what help is appropriate or available. An induction programme for new, first-time headteachers needs to pay particular attention to those problem situations where such help is important.

The main performance concerns of new staff are listed in the box below.

The performance concerns of new staff

How am I relating to my new colleagues?

How am I relating to my new pupils?

Am I developing efficient routines?

Am I dividing my time up appropriately between different tasks?

Am I ready to suggest changes to existing practices?

What image of myself am I projecting to others?

Am I communicating my needs clearly?

Have I made contact with those I need to?

Am I meeting my expectations?

Am I meeting the expectations of others?

Do I need help and advice?

Am I getting useful feedback on my performance?

How can I improve my performance?

Am I making best use of resources and support staff?

Am I meeting my key role responsibilities?

Am I getting overloaded with tasks?

Depending on your answers to these questions you can then think about how you can best deal with any concerns you have. In this respect, those who are in a position to provide you with helpful advice and guidance are of primary importance. It is very important for you to seek such help, as a lot of unnecessary pain and anguish can be prevented simply by being given appropriate help in good time rather than relying on trial and error. A trial and error approach tends to mean that it is only when problems have developed that you seek help, by which time avoidable stress may already have been generated for yourself and others.

Managing demands on staff

One of the most important things that school managers can do is to make sure that unnecessary demands are not made on staff. It is very easy when developing new practices and procedures in schools to require additional paperwork to be completed that may not in fact be necessary or could be more easily completed by clerical staff. Additional demands can also arise from adopting procedures that are unnecessarily time consuming and cumbersome to follow. For example, in compiling school reports it is important to ensure that each teacher can complete their part of the procedure in as easy and convenient a manner as possible. Teachers often find it very stressful to undertake a task that is unnecessarily time consuming when they feel the procedure could be made much easier.

Another source of additional demands on staff is allowing demanding activities to occur too close to each other. For example, if the deadline for completing school reports coincides with the school sports day or parents' evening or examination marking, then acute stress could be caused for many staff that could easily have been avoided by a better staggering of the times when these activities occurred.

A major source of stress for teachers is losing any non-contact time they have during the school week in which to carry out preparation work and complete assessment and administrative tasks. Anything that can be done to protect what non-contact time staff have is very important.

Staff also need to have an adequate level of resourcing and clerical and technical support for their work. Schools that have a good level of reprographic and technical support for staff will reduce much of the stress that is generated by pressure relating to preparation work.

Another important task for senior managers is to help match additional duties to the particular skills of individual teachers. Certain teachers are better able to do certain additional duties and feel more comfortable in some roles than in others. Thus, asking a teacher to take charge of organising the school prize day may be a real delight to one teacher but a real worry for another. It is important to ensure that the allocation to teachers of additional duties is as well fitted as possible to their skills and disposition.

Mills (1990) has highlighted 12 improvements that may help senior managers in a school reduce time pressures and workload for teachers. These are listed below.

- Set deadlines for reports well in advance.
- Ensure that the report system is clear, simple and efficient.
- Make marking and preparation time available during school hours.
- Ensure that future events are clearly displayed with ample warning time to prepare.
- Allow time for discussion with pupils and colleagues.
- Ensure that all meetings are essential and kept to an acceptable frequency and length.

- Appoint a staff member with responsibility for monitoring workload.
- Allow enough time on the timetable to achieve syllabus aims and goals.
- Keep general paperwork and administration to the absolute minimum.
- Ensure that teachers do not spend time on tasks that can be done by secretarial staff.
- Allocate adequate time for extra administrative responsibilities.
- Allocate time and staff help for records of achievement.

Another very important task for senior managers in a school is to ensure that there are whole-school policies in operation so that problems which can cause stress are kept to a minimum and teachers are clear about what action to take when problems arise.

The most important whole-school policy that can have an impact on reducing teacher stress is a whole-school policy on discipline. Indeed, some books on reducing teacher stress devote most of their text to ways in which teachers and schools can minimise discipline problems (e.g. Rogers, 1992). A whole-school policy on discipline should not simply be concerned with how to deal effectively with pupil misbehaviour. Rather it must also seek to establish and sustain good pupil behaviour. In other words, it seeks both to prevent problems and to deal with those that occur. Rogers (1992), for example, describes the essence of such a policy as being to state, as unambiguously as possible, how the school seeks to help pupils to behave responsibly.

The main benefit of having a whole-school policy on discipline is that it helps to ensure that teachers are acting in a consistent manner, and pupils can thereby develop a clear view of what behaviour is acceptable and what is not. When problems occur, the teacher will feel less isolated, and will be able to cite school expectations for good behaviour, rather than being uncertain as to whether they are personally being too strict or too lax regarding a particular type of incident. The teacher will also be clearer about the possible courses of action that can be taken if misbehaviour continues or is serious. A whole-school policy can additionally be helpful in designating roles to particular members of staff and in clarifying who is expected to monitor pupil behaviour in areas outside the classroom (such as in corridors or in the playground).

Establishing a whole-school policy on discipline can help generate a spirit of camaraderie and teamwork amongst staff, which can have positive benefits in contributing to an ethos of mutual support amongst colleagues in other aspects of their work.

There are also aspects of school life where, when problems are identified, they are difficult, perhaps even traumatising, for the teacher to deal with. For example, bullying in schools is a widespread problem, and causes a lot of suffering amongst pupils. Unfortunately, only a small fraction of such incidents are identified and dealt with successfully by teachers. Often you will have suspicions, but the bullied pupil may not come to you for help or wish to talk about their problems to you. It can be very upsetting to have such suspicions but feel unable to help. Similarly, if you suspect child abuse is occurring, you may find it very difficult and upsetting to have to voice your concerns. Another example of an area which teachers may find it difficult to deal with is a pupil's loss, through death or divorce, of a parent. In all such areas of sensitivity, the establishment of a whole-school policy on procedures to be followed, with designated role responsibilities together with advice and guidance for the teacher on what to do, can be very helpful in lessening the stress that may be generated.

Finally, it is very important for senior managers not to use their position to make unreasonable or excessive demands on staff. Each new task may in itself seem quite small, but, when added to other tasks, can gradually lead to teachers being overloaded. In addition, there are some tasks that require a large amount of time and effort, such as preparing for a school inspection by Ofsted. Careful and sensible planning of what needs to be done, by when and by whom, can make a vast difference to teachers' level of stress.

Enhancing staff morale

Enhancing staff morale is extremely important in mitigating the experience of stress. Teachers working in a school that can develop a real sense of purpose and team spirit will be better able to deal positively with the demands made upon them. School managers need to try to enhance staff morale by giving positive feedback and praise for work well done, and by keeping staff fully informed of important decisions affecting them. As noted in the previous section, the development of a whole-school policy on important matters can help establish a consensus amongst staff in the school which will do much to create a feeling of teamwork.

Staff morale can also be enhanced by teachers' perception of their school's image in the eyes of the local community. Efforts should therefore be made to ensure that good news about the school is made widely known and celebrated, and that from time to time such news appears in local newspapers.

The introduction of teacher appraisal is a very good example of a development that has the potential both to enhance staff morale and to undermine it. Research on teacher appraisal has shown that one of the major benefits for staff being appraised is that they received positive feedback on their performance. Indeed, in a study I conducted on teachers' experience of being appraised (Kyriacou, 1995), several teachers reported that after many years teaching in the school, their formal appraisal was the first time that anyone else in the school

Good publicity raises staff morale

had told them that the quality of their work was highly regarded and highly valued. Many teachers also appreciated having time set aside in which the problems they faced in doing their work and their professional development needs could be discussed with a view to positive action being taken to meet any needs identified.

In contrast, however, there were also teachers who reported finding the whole experience of being appraised very stressful, and who also felt that this form of 'checking up and evaluating their work' was an infringement of their autonomy which undermined their sense of professionalism. As one teacher said:

> I found the whole process very stressful. What bothers me is that at the heart of appraisal is the idea that teachers can't be trusted to do their work properly. In the past, if a teacher was having problems, they would get support and advice to help them improve. If the problems went on and were serious, they would be counselled to leave teaching. Why on earth every teacher in the whole country has to now spend hours and hours of their time being appraised or appraising someone else beats me. This is all time we ought to be spending doing what we are paid to do – teach!

The attempt to link teacher appraisal to performance-related pay is also a double-edged sword. On the one hand there are those who argue that such a linkage can enhance teachers' sense of professionalism and thereby increase staff morale. On the other hand, there are those who argue that it will inevitably be divisive and unfair in how it operates, and that staff morale will be seriously undermined.

Unfortunately, the procedures and processes which are put into operation for such schemes are normally tightly prescribed by the government, which means that schools have little room for manoeuvre in how such schemes operate. What schools can do, however, is to ensure that wherever possible, practices are followed which enhance staff morale as much as possible rather than undermine it. These include making sure that staff are fully informed about how such schemes will operate, and that the school is making as much effort as possible to ensure that they operate fairly.

If teachers feel that a scheme is well organised and that senior managers are 'on their side' in their attempts to implement it, then such a scheme may help enhance staff morale. If, however, staff feel the scheme is badly organised or that it is being used to pursue the senior managers' agenda in an unfair manner, then such a scheme is likely to undermine morale.

Staff morale very much depends on establishing a spirit of teamwork and camaraderie within a school. Teachers need to have a feeling of goodwill towards others in the school (both colleagues and pupils) if they are to give of their best. Anything that has the potential to be divisive must therefore be treated with extreme caution. This is particularly true of anything which involves making judgements or inferences about a teacher's professional competence, which is why teacher appraisal and performance-related pay are such controversial areas.

In a number of schools, a range of school events are used to bring staff together in a way that will enhance staff morale. Taking part in events such as school outings, school concerts or sports days offers an opportunity for staff to act together outside their normal classroom or staffroom setting. Such events can promote positive social exchanges amongst staff, and provide some useful critical distance from the everyday problems associated with classroom life.

In some schools, social events involving staff can help enhance morale. One school invited me to run a workshop on teacher stress on a staff training day based at a hotel which had a health and leisure club attached. As part of the training day, staff were encouraged to make use of the leisure facilities, which included a swimming pool, sauna, aromatherapy massage, and a golf drive machine. A good quality lunch was also provided. The day not only helped teachers to develop their coping strategies for dealing with stress, but also got them thinking about health and leisure activities. In addition, the setting provided a context for humorous banter, which undoubtedly helped to promote a more positive social climate amongst the staff.

Staff morale is also enhanced by feeling that you are being treated as a professional and with respect. Teachers often think about how other professionals are treated. This is illustrated by the followed comment:

> I know I need to go on an in-service course – in fact it's written into my appraisal statement. However, I've just been told that the school budget won't be able to cover my fees for the course I want to take. I could pay the fees myself and it will involve giving up one evening a week for nine weeks. I can't think of many professions where you are expected to give up your own time and pay for your own training. I think this is laughable if it wasn't so sad.

This sense of self-image is extremely important to staff morale. Quite simple things, like the provision by one school of freshly baked scones at minimum cost every morning break time, or by another of tea and coffee during parents' evenings, all help you to feel that your well-being is being cared for. By contrast, the absence of simple things, like not enough armchairs in the staffroom for everyone to be able to sit down, or long queues to use a photocopying machine, makes you feel undervalued and as if everything is an uphill struggle. Paying attention to teachers' working conditions, by making sure that staff facilities are well cared for, can have a major impact on enhancing staff morale.

Establishing a climate of support

A study by Johnstone (1993) asked teachers in primary and secondary schools to keep a workload diary for one week (Sunday to Saturday inclusive) which divided the day into 15-minute intervals. At the end of each day the teachers were asked to report on whether they had felt stressed during the day and what they had done to deal with the stress. During the school week, a major coping strategy reported by these teachers was receiving support from colleagues in school who helped by sharing the burden. Senior staff who were supportive also received particular praise.

The report of the Education Service Advisory Committee (1998) has highlighted a number of ways in which senior mangers could help develop a supportive culture in schools:

- ensuring they are accessible to staff to discuss problems and anxieties
- taking a lead in changing the view that being under stress is a reflection of personal vulnerability
- developing effective induction and introduction programmes for new staff

- encouraging staff to talk about feelings and the effects of stress
- encouraging, commending and recognising supportive behaviour in others
- developing cooperative rather than adversarial management styles
- engendering team spirit, a sense of belonging and sharing aims and objectives
- recognising that people may be worried about returning to work after sickness absence, and providing support
- encouraging staff to make use of confidential occupational health advice.

Teachers in a school need to feel that when they are having problems, there is a climate of support in the school which will try to help them resolve these problems. This means that when school managers are approached by colleagues who point to difficulties they are facing, they will deal sympathetically with the colleague and try to take whatever positive action they can to deal with the problem raised.

Teachers need to feel valued

Another important aspect of establishing a climate of support is that staff are able to relax together. Good facilities in the staffroom for relaxation, tea and coffee, and work preparation areas, can help immensely in establishing such a climate.

Some additional support and advice can also be provided through professional development activities, including teacher appraisal. These can offer teachers opportunities to review their work practices and to highlight problems that can be resolved, with or without additional support.

Where conflicts have occurred between staff, senior managers have an important part to play in ensuring that these are resolved speedily and amicably so that a spirit of collegiality is re-established. Where the conflict is between a senior manager and a colleague, this again needs to be resolved quickly.

The point is often made that each school has its own unique organisational climate. An important part of this is how teachers feel they are seen and valued by senior managers in the school, and the extent to which they feel their needs and concerns are properly taken into account when important decisions affecting work practices are made. An atmosphere of consultation and negotiation will help establish a supportive climate in the school. However, if the senior managers, particularly the headteacher, are regarded as being abrasive and inconsiderate, this will undoubtedly generate more stress for teachers.

Beginning teachers certainly need support during the induction year, and school mentors can help provide this. However, it is also important to regard any change in role as needing support, and the extension of the mentor model to apply to any promoted post can also help to alleviate stress.

A number of writers and teacher unions have also advocated that teachers should have good access to counselling services (Education Service Advisory Committee, 1998). In the case of large schools, such services could be provided in a school on a regular basis by a peripatetic counsellor serving a group of large schools. Such a person would be in a position to listen to a teacher's concerns and to offer advice on direct-action and palliative strategies that the teacher could use. Counsellors can be particularly effective in alerting teachers to bad mental habits they have developed, which may have contributed to increasing their level of stress. They may also be in a position themselves to help teachers to learn how to use strategies that normally require some degree of training, such as time management, assertiveness, meditation, breathing exercises, improving voice and posture, and guided imagery. A counsellor would also be in a position to advise the teacher on whether medical attention should be sought, for example if a teacher has reported experiencing panic attacks from time to time, or having chest pains.

Huberman (1993) estimated that about 40 per cent of teachers encounter one or more periods in their careers when they feel that the stress of teaching is so great that they may be unable to continue. This may be triggered by problems with a particularly difficult class, or by problems stemming from personal and family events at home. For the vast majority of teachers, this period is short lived, perhaps lasting only a few weeks, and they decide to continue with their career as a teacher. For some, however, it lasts longer, is more intense, and eventually precipitates the decision to leave the profession. Counsellors might well be in a position to offer particular help to teachers during such periods to deal with these feelings more effectively.

A particularly interesting example of counselling is the use of a counsellor in the period leading up to an Ofsted inspection. One teacher reported the following experience:

> In my primary school the LEA paid for a counsellor to be in the school for the whole of the week immediately prior to our Ofsted inspection. The counsellor spent most of the time sitting in the staff room listening to us moaning about the problems we were facing. She occasionally offered advice, but generally just listened and acted sympathetically. Her presence was a great help. I think because we were all so stressed, there was little point just moaning to each other all the time. By having someone there who you could talk to and who would be sympathetic meant we could all get things off our chest. The counsellor was an experienced teacher from another school who had gone through Ofsted inspections herself, so she knew and understood what we were all going through. I know the LEA have paid for her to do this at quite a few schools now, so they obviously think this is a great help. I certainly found it so.

Interestingly, with regard to Ofsted inspections, many teachers have told me that the long period of advance notice given to schools does much to increase the stress generated. A teacher at a school that was given two terms' advance warning told me:

> We were told what term the inspection was to occur in two terms in advance, and we were given the precise week about three months in advance. I think we were given much too much warning, and the stress just gradually built up and up. I would be in favour of two weeks' warning. That would mean false expectations would not be created and the inspection would be over with before people started dropping like ninepins with stress. With a long lead-in time, you just get the feeling that if you're not perfect in every respect, you'll get hammered.

Whilst there is a responsibility on senior mangers in schools to help establish a climate of support for teachers, a number of writers have raised the issue of whose responsibility it is to support the needs of the senior managers themselves, and in particular the needs of the headteacher. In a study of stress amongst headteachers, Cooper and Kelly (1993) argued that local education authorities needed to take the lead in establishing support systems for head-teachers, which should include counselling services. In addition, they felt that a programme of mid-career development for headteachers was essential in order to avoid managerial burnout. Given the above comment, it is not surpris-ing that a number of headteachers have also requested counselling support for themselves in the run-up to Ofsted inspections.

Professional development activities

In order to help teachers to deal with new developments and changes that they face in their work, it is essential that professional development activities are organised on a regular basis. These include meetings and workshops for the staff as a whole as well as more specialised activities for individuals or small groups of staff within the school. An important aspect of such activities is that they also help to develop a sense of collegiality and teamwork amongst teach-ers. It is also important that when teachers are involved in such activities, they feel they are being treated in a professional manner. Meetings that are well

Keeping up to date is important

organised and which take place in comfortable settings away from the school can help enhance such feelings. A poorly organised activity, even if the content is good, may do little to enhance staff morale.

Another important aspect of such activities is that they should be seen as positive in nature and with respect to professional enhancement, and not couched in a way that suggests that current practice is poor and must change.

A number of schools have also included workshops on stress management in their programme of professional development activities. Such activities tend to work best if they involve an outside organiser, and if the activity covers both what individuals can do to cope better with stress and the action that senior managers in the school can take to deal with problems that are identified. Individual teachers may also arrange to attend stress-management workshops arranged for teachers from different schools. This has the benefit of ensuring anonymity, and can encourage some teachers to be more honest about the problems they are facing. Indeed, in a survey of teacher stress workshops, Seidman and Zager (1992) noted that workshops that were held away from school premises in an environment that would help participants to relax and which involved a mix of teachers from different schools tended to be particularly productive and effective.

Many stress-management workshops also include a session on relaxation training and emotional control techniques. It is surprising how many teachers who report experiencing a high level of stress have not actively thought about how they can use various coping techniques to deal with stress.

In some schools, the member of staff in charge of professional development activities can play a key role in alerting some teachers to the need not to become a workaholic, and to develop an approach to their work that is more realistic and sustainable over a long period. Sometimes this advice can come from an appraiser, a mentor, or simply a colleague. It is important, however, for school managers to be alert to whether some teachers are simply taking on too much and to counsel them appropriately.

Professional development activities, however, can also have negative aspects. In particular, it is important that the activity is seen by teachers to be relevant to their needs. Many teachers complain that they have attended INSET activities that were a waste of time.

Because teachers are often under pressure with tasks that need attention, it is very easy for them to feel that a particular professional development activity that they are required to attend does not address their own personal agenda of needs and at the same time deprives them of time that could more usefully be spent attending to other tasks. It is thus easy for them in this situation to feel frustrated and resentful. Therefore, when organising professional development activities, it is essential that staff at the school have an influence on the choice of activities. In addition, when they are required to attend an activity which they might have doubts about, it is essential that senior managers explain the need for this activity, such as, for example, how the activity will help staff prepare for particular changes that will be occurring or help the school to meet legal obligations in an aspect of their work.

Dealing with problems

In every school there are problems and issues that arise from time to time that create stress for teachers, which can be dealt with by senior managers. In many cases, resolving these can make a marked impact on reducing stress. For example, there may be concerns in the school that a new format for the school timetable has not adequately taken into account the problems of working on a split site; the presence of a gang of pupils from a neighbouring school may have led to some ugly incidents occurring at the end of the school day; and some teachers may have complained about the workings of the teacher appraisal scheme. When such problems have been identified, it is very important for senior managers to take appropriate action. When problems are not easily dealt with, it is useful to inform teachers of this, so that they at least know that the problem is recognised and that steps are being taken to do what is possible.

Three areas in particular are worthy of note. The first deals with the physical demands made on teachers in their work. Having to climb up flights of stairs carrying books and equipment will pose major problems for some teachers. Senior managers need to think very carefully about the physical demands made on teachers which stem from the built environment and the tasks teachers have to carry out. It is very easy to take such activities for granted, and to overlook ways in which physical demands can be minimised. For example, it is very helpful to have areas about the school where books and equipment can be kept near to where they will be used.

The second area of particular note is the noise level in the school. Some schools have building characteristics which seem to enhance noise levels. In addition, the signalling system used to mark the beginning and ending of lessons, such as a ringing bell, can be very loud. Efforts to minimise noise levels, such as carpeting and other sound-proofing, can help to develop a pleasant working environment and have a marked impact on reducing levels of stress.

The third area of particular note concerns trying to prevent stagnation. Many teachers are very happy to stay working in the same school for a long period, and may have little desire to change school or seek promotion. At the same time, there are other teachers who may have made unsuccessful efforts to move school or gain promotion, and who may feel somewhat frustrated as a result. For both groups of teachers, there is a danger that doing the same job over and over again, with little change or variety, can lead to stagnation. One of the positive characteristics of the teaching profession, however, is that there is the opportunity to generate variety in your work in a number of different ways. This may involve making changes in the topic areas and age groups taught, changes in administrative duties, changes in teaching methods, doing educational research for a higher degree, organising a school trip, and taking on more pastoral care responsibilities. Senior managers can play an active part in encouraging teachers to consider ways in which they can add variety to their work in these ways, in order to keep teachers feeling continually refreshed.

Finally, there are one-off demands that are serious and wide ranging in their effects. These include the high-level stress that is generated by major reorganisations, such as when one school merges with another school, or radically changes its status and pupil intake. Other examples are personal tragedies, such as when a pupil or teacher is killed; or a school catching fire. Such one-off demands can be traumatising for all those involved, and great care and sensitivity needs to be brought into play in order to help those involved deal with these experiences and their aftermath. For example, Shears (1995) outlines how one school coped with the aftermath of a tragedy as news emerged that the ship carrying pupils and teachers from the school and two nearby schools had sunk in the Mediterranean. It was eventually reported that one pupil and one teacher in the party had been lost, presumed drowned. Some local education authorities have recognised the need to provide emergency counselling support during such periods, but there is a real need for such provision to become more widespread and sustained than is typically the case in many parts of the country.

School action to minimise stress

Use Table 6.1 to list five actions you feel the school could take to minimise stress for you personally and five actions the school could take to minimise stress for other teachers in your school. Consider how you could feed these ideas into managerial decision making in your school. This might include raising ideas for such action during the teacher appraisal process, staff development workshops, staff meetings or directly with the headteacher or another senior teacher. There is an increasing expectation that schools will take appropriate action to minimise teacher stress, and the free flow of suggestions from staff on how to do this can play an important part in achieving this successfully.

Table 6.1 School action to minimise stress

Do this!

List below five actions you feel the school could take to minimise stress for you personally.

1 _____

2 _____

3 _____

4 _____

5 _____

List below five actions you feel the school could take to minimise stress for other teachers in your school.

1 _____

2 _____

3 _____

4 _____

5 _____

7 Taking action *now*!

Having reached the end of this book you are faced with the most important decision you can take concerning reducing your level of stress. The decision is to commit yourself to taking action *now*!

In reading this book, you have looked at the nature of stress and considered a range of effective strategies that can be used to reduce stress. If you leave things there, you will certainly gain some benefits. A better understanding of stress on its own will help reduce stress. This is because understanding what is happening to you and being aware of the causes and processes involved in itself will give you a greater feeling of control over your situation. It is often not knowing or understanding why you are experiencing stress that drastically enhances the feeling of stress.

However, to really gain the benefit of the strategies outlined in this book you have to commit yourself to devoting some time to thinking about and planning what strategies you will use.

Dealing with stress can quickly create a virtuous circle. The more effectively you deal with stress, the more time and effort you will have to deal with new demands, and the better you will feel, and this in turn will mean that new demands are much less likely to pose any problems for you. Of course, if things were as easy as that, why is it that some teachers fail to take positive action to deal with stress?

One problem is that dealing with stress requires time and effort, and when you are experiencing stress, time and effort is often the last thing you feel you have available. In reading this book you have already taken a positive step towards more effective coping, and you are now in a very good position to take the action needed to gain the maximum benefit.

Another problem is that some people are reluctant to admit to others that they experience stress, not only at work to colleagues at work, but even at home to their spouse and friends. There is sometimes a fear that admitting to stress in part suggests that you are failing, and indeed that it may undermine the regard in which you are held by others. Whilst it is true that in some schools senior managers and colleagues may be less supportive than would be ideal, in the vast majority of schools it is recognised that helping colleagues to deal effectively with stress is part of aiding good professional development. Those teachers who do not recognise their problems are doing themselves no favours. In fact, they are undermining their own opportunity for important professional development. In addition, a number of studies have indicated that those who are reluctant to seek social support by talking about their stress to others are more likely to experience prolonged stress and to suffer stress-related ill health as a consequence (Forbes and Roger, 1999).

Having committed yourself to developing more effective coping strategies in a determined way, you have every chance of enhancing your effectiveness and gaining more satisfaction from your work. Start *now* by developing an action plan of what you are going to do in the immediate future (over the next week) and in the longer term (over the next few months) to reduce stress. Then commit yourself to review your action on a regular basis, say once a month, to take stock of how successful your action has been, and to consider what new action you need to take. You should also re-read parts of this book, as the issues and strategies described will generate new ideas for you each time your context and circumstances change.

Finally, you need to remember that only you can really help yourself. Your opportunity to keep your stress to a minimum simply lies with you.

Take action now!

Bibliography

Benmansour, N. (1998). 'Job satisfaction, stress and coping strategies among Moroccan high school teachers.' *Mediterranean Journal of Educational Studies*, vol. 3, pp. 13–33.

Borg, M. G. (1990). 'Occupational stress in British educational settings: a review.' *Educational Psychology,* vol. 10, pp. 103–26.

Borg, M. G. and Falzon, J. M. (1990). 'Coping actions by Maltese primary school teachers.' *Educational Research,* vol. 32, pp. 50–8.

Borg, M. G. and Riding, R. J. (1993). 'Teacher stress and cognitive style.' *British Journal of Educational Psychology*, vol. 63, pp. 271–6.

Bowers, T. (1995). 'Teacher stress and assertiveness as a coping mechanism.' *Research in Education*, no. 53, pp. 24–30.

Cains, R. A. and Brown, C. R. (1998). 'Newly qualified teachers: a comparative analysis of the perceptions held by B.Ed. and PGCE-trained primary teachers of the level and frequency of stress experienced during the first year of teaching.' *Educational Psychology*, vol. 18, pp. 97–110.

Cartwright, S. and Cooper, C. L. (1997). *Managing Workplace Stress*. London: Sage.

Cherniss, C. (1995). *Beyond Burnout: Helping Teachers, Nurses, Therapists and Lawyers Recover from Stress and Disillusionment*. London: Routledge.

Cockburn, A. D. (1996a). 'Primary teachers' knowledge and acquisition of stress relieving strategies.' *British Journal of Educational Psychology*, vol. 66, pp. 399–410.

Cockburn, A. D. (1996b). *Teaching under Pressure: Looking at Primary Teachers' Stress*. London: Falmer.

Cole, M. and Walker, S. (eds) (1989). *Teaching and Stress*. Milton Keynes: Open University Press.

Cooper, C. L. and Kelly, M. (1993). 'Occupational stress in head teachers: a national UK study.' *British Journal of Educational Psychology*, vol. 63, pp. 130–43.

Dunham, J. (1976). 'Stress situations and responses.' In NAS/UWT, *Stress in Schools*. Hemel Hempstead: NAS/UWT.

Dunham, J. (1992). *Stress in Teaching* (2nd edition). London: Routledge.

Dunham, J. and Varma, V. (eds) (1998). *Stress in Teachers: Past, Present and Future*. London: Whurr.

Education Service Advisory Committee (1998). *Managing Work-related Stress: A Guide for Managers and Teachers in the Schools* (2nd edition). London: HMSO.

Fontana, D. (1989). *Managing Stress*. London: Routledge/BPS.

Fontana, D. and Abouserie, R. (1993). 'Stress levels, gender and personality factors in teachers.' *British Journal of Educational Psychology*, vol. 63, pp. 261–70.

Forbes, A. and Roger, D. (1999). 'Stress, social support and fear of disclosure.' *British Journal of Health Psychology*, vol. 4, pp. 165–79.

Gold, Y. and Roth, R. A. (1993). *Teachers Managing Stress and Preventing Burnout: The Professional Health Solution*. London: Falmer Press.

Gray, H. and Freeman, A. (1987). *Teaching Without Stress*. London: Paul Chapman.

Greene, R. W., Abidin, R. R. and Kmetz, C. (1997). 'The index of teaching stress: a measure of student–teacher compatibility.' *Journal of School Psychology*, vol. 35, pp. 239–59.

Guglielmi, R. S. and Tatrow, K. (1998). 'Occupational stress, burnout and health in teachers: a methodological and theoretical analysis.' *Review of Educational Research*, vol. 68, pp. 61–99.

Head, J., Hill, F. and Maguire, M. (1996). 'Stress and the postgraduate secondary school trainee teacher: a British case study.' *Journal of Education for Teaching*, vol. 22, pp. 71–84.

Health Education Authority (1988). *Stress in the Public Sector: Nurses, Police, Social Workers and Teachers*. London: Health Education Authority.

Huberman, M. (1993). *The Lives of Teachers*. London: Cassell.

Jeffrey, B. and Woods, P. (1996). 'Feeling deprofessionalised: the social construction of emotions during an OFSTED inspection.' *Cambridge Journal of Education*, vol. 26, pp. 325–44.

Johnstone, M. (1993). *Time and Tasks: Teacher Workload and Stress* (Spotlights 44). Edinburgh: Scottish Council for Research in Education.

Jones, D. and Sharma, D. (1996). 'Learning difficulties.' In Upton, G. and Varma, V. (eds) *Stresses in Special Educational Needs Teachers*. Aldershot: Arena.

Kremer-Hayon, L. and Kurtz, J. E. (1985). 'The relation of personal and environmental variables to teacher burnout.' *Teaching and Teacher Education*, vol. 1, pp. 243–9.

Kyriacou, C. (1995). 'An evaluation of teacher appraisal in schools within one local education authority.' *School Organisation*, vol. 15, pp. 109–16.

Kyriacou, C. (1998). *Essential Teaching Skills* (2nd edition). Cheltenham: Stanley Thornes.

Kyriacou, C. and Harriman, P. (1993). 'Teacher stress and school merger.' *School Organisation*, vol. 13, pp. 297–302.

Kyriacou, C. and Pratt, J. (1985). 'Teacher stress and psychoneurotic symptoms.' *British Journal of Educational Psychology*, vol. 55, pp. 61–4.

Kyriacou, C. and Stephens, P. (1999). 'Student teachers' concerns during teaching practice.' *Evaluation and Research in Education*, vol. 13, pp. 18–31.

Kyriacou, C. and Sutcliffe, J. (1978a). 'A model of teacher stress.' *Educational Studies*, vol. 4, pp. 1–6.

Kyriacou, C. and Sutcliffe, J. (1978b). 'Teacher stress: prevalence, sources and symptoms.' *British Journal of Educational Psychology*, vol. 48, pp. 159–67.

Lloyd, S. R. (1995). *Developing Positive Assertiveness*. Menlo Park, California: Crisp Publications.

Mills, S. H. (1990). *Stress Management for Teachers*. Lancaster: Framework Press.

Mills, S. H. (1995). *Stress Management for the Individual Teacher*. Lancaster: Framework Press.

Morton, L. L., Vesco, R., Williams, N. H. and Awender, M. A. (1997). 'Student teacher anxieties related to class management, pedagogy, evaluation, and staff relations.' *British Journal of Educational Psychology*, vol. 67, pp. 69–89.

NUT (1990). *Health and Safety: Teachers, Stress and Schools.* London: National Union of Teachers.

Ostell, A. and Oakland, S. (1995). *Headteacher Stress, Coping and Health.* Aldershot: Avebury.

Pithers, R. T. and Soden, R. (1998). 'Scottish and Australian teacher stress and strain: a comparative study.' *British Journal of Educational Psychology*, vol. 68, pp. 269–79.

Pithers, R. T. and Soden, R. (1999). 'Person-environment fit and teacher stress.' *Educational Research*, vol. 41, pp. 51–61.

Punch, K. F. and Tuetteman, E. (1996). 'Reducing teacher stress; the effects of support in the work environment.' *Research in Education*, no. 56, pp. 63–72.

Roger, D. and Hudson, C. (1995). 'The role of emotion control and emotional rumination in stress management training.' *International Journal of Stress Management*, vol. 2, pp. 119–32.

Rogers, B. (1992). *Managing Teacher Stress.* London: Pitman.

Salo, K. (1995). 'Teacher-stress processes: how can they be explained?' *Scandinavian Journal of Educational Research*, vol. 39, pp. 205–22.

Seidman, S. A. and Zager, J. (1992). 'Teacher stress workshops.' *Work and Stress*, vol. 6, pp. 85–7.

Shears, J. (1995). 'Managing a tragedy in a secondary school.' In Smith, S. C. and Pennells, M. (eds) *Interventions with Bereaved Children.* London: Jessica Kingsley.

Sheffield, D., Dobbie, D. and Carroll, D. (1994). 'Stress, social support, and psychological and physical wellbeing in secondary school teachers.' *Work and Stress*, vol. 8, pp. 235–43.

Teacher Training Agency (1999). *Induction for Newly Qualified Teachers.* London: TTA.

Travers, C. J. and Cooper, C. L. (1996). *Teachers under Pressure: Stress in the Teaching Profession.* London: Routledge.

Upton, G. and Varma, V. (eds.) (1996). *Stresses in Special Educational Needs Teachers.* Aldershot: Arena.

Van Horn, J. E., Schaufeli, W. B. and Enzmann, D. (1999). 'Teacher burnout and lack of reciprocity.' *Journal of Applied Social Psychology*, vol. 29, pp. 91–108.

Wilson, P. (1998). *Calm at Work.* London: Penguin.

Author index

Subject index